6-16-76

THE WORLD NATURALIST

The Natural History of the Horse

The Natural History of the Horse

John Clabby

TAPLINGER PUBLISHING COMPANY
New York

First published in the United States in 1976 by
TAPLINGER PUBLISHING CO., INC.
New York, New York

Library of Congress Catalog Card Number: 75-33426
ISBN 0-8008-5467-5

Contents

Plates

Acknowledgements for photographs

The publishers acknowledge with thanks the permission of the following to reproduce photographs: the Mansell Collection, plate 1; the Zoological Society of London, plates 2, 3, 4, 7, 8, 9; Radio Times Hulton Picture Library, plates 5, 10, 18, 22; Sally Anne Thompson (Animal Photography Ltd), plates 6, 11, 12, 13, 19, 20(b), 21, 28, 29, 30, 31, 32, 33, 34; Fores Ltd, plates 15, 16; Novosti Press Agency, plates 17, 20(a), 23, 24, 25, 26, 27.

Figures

Foreword by L. Harrison Matthews

THE horse has been almost entirely ousted from working for man in the western world by the internal combustion engine. On the other hand with his relief from drudgery he gains an ever increasing popularity for healthy recreation, for is not the best thing for the inside of a man the outside of a horse? The rapidly growing number of riders and other horse enthusiasts will find this book an absorbing account of the history, life, and relations of the friend of man.

Few can be better qualified to write the natural history of the horse than Brigadier John Clabby. He was born in India and educated at Taunton School and the Royal Veterinary College, London. After qualifying as MRCVS in 1932 he was commissioned as a lieutenant in the Royal Army Veterinary Corps, and spent the years until 1939 mostly with Indian Cavalry regiments on the North-West Frontier where he saw active service in two frontier operations. He was back in England at the outbreak of World War II and went with 9,000 horses of the 1st Cavalry Division to Palestine. Thence he went to Eritrea with two pack mule companies where he took part in the siege of Cheren. In April 1941 he took a veterinary hospital to Greece to provide support for the pack transport of troops fighting the Germans in the mountains, but was taken prisoner and spent the rest of the war in prisoner-of-war camps.

After the war he served as Lt Colonel in India for two years until the Partition, and then in the Middle East and the Far East. On coming home he was posted first to the War Office and then to the RAVC Depot at Melton Mowbray, and was Director of the Army Veterinary and Remount Services 1959–63. On retiring he joined the Equine Research Station of the Animal Health Trust at Newmarket, and then became Chief Executive Officer of the Trust at its London headquarters where he now is. Brigadier Clabby went in for polo and show jumping when he was abroad, and at home he has hunted whenever possible with the Quorn, Belvoir, and Worcestershire packs. He is Colonel Commandant of the Royal Army Veterinary Corps, and is a Past-Master of the Worshipful Company of Farriers, and Past-President of the British Equine Veterinary Association; he wrote the *History of the RAVC 1919–1961*, which was published in 1961.

A glance at the chapter headings on the contents page of this book shows the wide scope of treatment that Brigadier Clabby has brought to his subject. He traces the evolution of the horse and its relatives through an immense period of time from their earliest known ancestors in the Paleocene epoch over sixty million years ago. He then describes the wild horses, asses, onagers, and zebras of recent times—many species greatly reduced from their former abundance and apparently nearing extinction. When he comes to the origin of the domestic horse, and of the many different breeds that have been developed for various purposes by man, Brigadier Clabby gives us an immense amount of fascinating information that will rivet the attention of all naturalists as well as devotees of the horse. His chapter on the social behaviour of the equids incorporates the results of the latest researches in the growing science of ethology, and that on horse breeding is based on the modern knowledge of genetics developed since the discovery of the 'double helix' and the structure of deoxyribonucleic acid, DNA, the physical basis of heredity. His final chapter on the horse-crafts fittingly concludes the work with a discussion of the evolution of the management of horses by man through the ages.

This book by a lifelong horseman is an admirable natural history that gives the reader whether general naturalist or horse enthusiast a most readable account of the animal that has played a more important part than any other in human history. It is a most welcome addition to the World Naturalist Series.

Chapter 1

Perspective

THE horse family, Equidae, includes horses, asses, onagers and zebras. It is with these animals and their ancestors that this book is concerned. When discussing the history of the ancestors, which can be traced back through the fossil record for many millions of years, frequent reference will be made to the geological time scale shown in table 1. It will be noted that the narrative stretches over virtually the whole of the Cenozoic, the age of mammals, which embraces both the Tertiary and the Quaternary periods and continues to the present day.

Table 1. Geological Time Scale

Era	Period	Epoch	Approximate time before present, in millions of years
	Quaternary	Recent	
		Pleistocene	3
Cenozoic	Tertiary	Pliocene	7
		Miocene	26
		Oligocene	38
		Eocene	54
		Paleocene	65
Mesozoic		Cretaceous	135
		Jurassic	190
		Triassic	230

The family Equidae is one of the three now constituting the order Perissodactyla that contained fourteen families during the Tertiary. The other two survivors are the families Rhinocerotidae and Tapiridae.

Some of the characteristics shared by the horses, rhinoceroses and tapirs are that all are herbivorous and have dentitions suited to browsing or grazing; and all are hoofed animals that take the main weight of the body on the third digit of their limbs: a feature that clearly distinguishes them from the Artiodactyla or cloven-footed animals.

It is typical of the Perissodactyls that, in the course of evolution, the number of digits on each limb was reduced from the original mammalian five, which man still retains, to one toe in the case of modern horses, in rhinoceroses to three or four on the fore-limbs and three on the hind, while the tapirs persist with the limb form of their early ancestors, having four hoofed and padded toes on each fore-foot and three on each hind.

The ancestral Perissodactyls appeared during the Eocene and the fossil record of that epoch provides evidence that the earliest direct equine ancestor, namely *Hyracotherium* also called *Eohippus* or the dawn horse, was then abundant both in Europe and in North America. It was clearly a highly successful species, perfectly adapted to an existence in the tropical and semi-tropical forests that then covered much of the northern hemisphere. Nevertheless its descendants proved capable of evolving into animals that were equally successful in the very different environment of the ensuing epochs. In fact the changes in geography, climate and vegetation that took place were so marked that inevitably they influenced many forms of animal life.

The following brief survey outlines the main alterations in the environment during the Tertiary and Quaternary affecting the development of Equidae. Australia receives no mention because it is fairly certain that hoofed animals did not reach that island continent until settlers introduced their domestic stock in recent times.

South America was also once an island. And for most of the Tertiary, protected by this isolation, horse-like creatures evolved there from ancestors quite distinct from the eohippus line; they developed specialized limbs and teeth similar to those of horses and they occupied the same sort of ecological niche as those animals. Then, in the Pliocene, the joining of South America to the North by the Isthmus of Panama permitted a faunal interchange between the two continents. By the Pleistocene true horses from the north had replaced their South American counterparts, which then became extinct.

Africa was little affected by the extensive mountain building that disturbed so much of the world during the Tertiary and Pleistocene and its climate remained relatively stable. Cracraft [13] suggests that Africa could have had Tertiary climates similar to those of today and adds that in the north the continent was probably more humid than now and forest-covered. After the Miocene communication with Eurasia seldom seems to have been a problem. With the coming of the Ice Age many species retreated to Africa, some, such as the zebras, making it their permanent habitat and a few, such as hippopotami and hyenas, returning north again during the warm interglacials [Romer 49].

Tertiary Europe was a peninsular area forming a continuous land mass with Asia and both were connected with North America for most of the Tertiary and the Pleistocene by a land bridge across the Bering Straits.

At the beginning of the Tertiary there were none of the sharp temperature gradients between the poles and the equator that are so familiar today. Tropical forests extended as far north as Alaska. Cracraft [13] considers that similar forests may have existed over much of eastern Canada, Greenland and Scandinavia and that the warm broad-leaved forest was continuous over north-western North America and Asia at this period.

Then the temperatures started a marked trend downwards; at the same time the seas regressed exposing new coastlines; and great new mountain ranges – the Himalayas, the Alps, the Rockies, the Andes and others – built up over the previously flat lands.

The cooler drier weather that ensued changed the character of the tree covering, reduced the continuity and vastness of the forest area and drove the tree-line further south. Eventually in the late Miocene and Pliocene, a grassland environment was created and the prairies, pampas, steppes and savannas came into being.

Still the cold increased until the glacial phases of the Pleistocene were reached. Romer [49] summarizes the development of the glaciations of the Ice Age as follows:

Their boundaries fluctuated considerably during the course of the Pleistocene. The evidence indicates that there were four successive southward advances of the ice caps which covered much of Europe and North America. Contemporaneous with these advances were the development of great areas of tundra, local glaciations in more southerly mountain masses, and a shifting of climatic zones so that areas such as the Sahara and the deserts of the south-western United States were, for the time, well watered. Between the periods of glaciation there were three interglacial stages, during which zonal boundaries shifted far to the

3

north, so that essentially tropical conditions were to be found over great parts of Europe and North America.

Throughout the Tertiary, North America was the main home of the family Equidae and it was there that by the end of the Pliocene *Equus* evolved, the genus of the modern Equidae. *Equus* spread to South America and into Eurasia and was abundant throughout the New World and the Old during the Pleistocene. It was in the Old World of this period that *Equus* must have made its first significant contact with man.

It is likely that man originated in Africa during the Pliocene and spread to Eurasia during the Pleistocene. He depended greatly on game for food and his earlier stone tools seem to have been designed for the skinning of carcases. His hunting methods no doubt progressed from the stalking of individual animals with wooden spears to trapping numbers of them in pitfalls or with other devices; such trapping techniques would have been particularly applicable to easily stampeded herds of horses. Certainly in Europe horse flesh often formed a large proportion of man's diet. Kurten [33] points out that different tribes had different favourite game; some preferred mammoth, others reindeer and others specialized in horse hunting to such an extent that their middens contain the remains of thousands of wild horses. Despite these depredations herds of wild horses continued to roam Eurasia into recent times.

In America it was a different story. Towards the end of the Ice Age man crossed the Bering Straits land bridge and penetrated into the Americas. At about the same period the horse became extinct in both North and South America. It is suspicious that this extinction should coincide with man's arrival but neither the theory of over-hunting, a high mortality owing to some virulent equine epidemic nor any of the many other suggested explanations can be substantiated. It remains an unsolved mystery.

The gradual melting of the huge ice sheets of the last glaciation caused, among other things, the inundation of low coastal areas, a warmer rainier climate in Europe favourable to the spread of forests; and a drier climate in Africa and Asia that turned former fertile zones into deserts. Oakley [45] suggests that these happenings led to the migration of the game herds and a reduction in their size, creating a situation of game scarcity that made the life of the Stone-Age hunter very precarious indeed. Certainly from then on hunting declined in importance and a culture based on crop production and the breeding and rearing of animals spread from its places of origin in the Middle East to Europe and elsewhere.

Cole [11] says there is evidence of a very primitive type of agricultural settlement with domestic sheep in Iraq as long ago as 8900 BC, some six hundred years before the ending of the glacial conditions in Europe, and it seems certain that sheep and goats were among the first animals to be domesticated, perhaps preceded by the dog. The domestication of cattle and pigs came later, and later still the domestication of the ass and onager. Last of all came the horse, which around 3000 BC seems to have replaced the onager as a draught animal. The onager is not very tractable and like the zebras, which never took kindly to domestication, exists now only in the wild or in zoological collections.

In contrast the great majority of horses and asses are in domesticity and their story becomes largely one of the diversification of the species into breeds to suit man's varied requirements for work and recreation.

Chapter 2

The Ancestors

THE horse's earliest ancestor little resembled the modern horse. When, in 1839, its fossil bones were first disinterred from the London clay beds they were mistaken for those of a cony or hyrax, a rabbit-like creature, to which the name *Hyracotherium* was therefore allotted. Many years were to pass before *Hyracotherium* was recognized as the founder member of the family Equidae.

Mitchell [41] in his biography of T. H. Huxley records that in 1870 the eminent scientist delivered an address to the Geological Society of London in which he showed that there was a series of fossils tracing back the ancestry of the horse to a three-toed pony-sized animal of the Miocene, called *Anchitherium*, and argued that there must be older fossils leading still further back towards the common mammalian type of animal with five digits. Six years later Huxley visited America, apparently intending to give a similar lecture in New York.

However, before speaking, he took the opportunity to examine a comprehensive collection of American Tertiary fossils in the Yale Museum and what he saw there persuaded him to carry his thesis a stage further with the statement:

The European pedigree stops in the Miocene; in the American Tertiary, on the contrary, the series of equine ancestral forms is carried into the Eocene formations . . . the most important discovery of all is the *Orohippus* which is the oldest member of the equine series yet known. Here we find four complete toes on the fore limb, three toes on the hind limb, a well-developed fibula and short crowned grinders of a simple pattern.

As in his London lecture he went on to predict the finding of types of even greater antiquity. One of these was indeed discovered before his lecture had gone into print and he was able to add in a footnote some

6

details of a small creature which, because it was found in the early Eocene beds, was named *Eohippus*. Later it was recognized that this belonged to the same genus as *Hyracotherium*.

Eohippus appears quite suddenly in the Eocene with its Perissodactyl characteristics already clearly defined. No obvious ancestor precedes it in the fossil record but fairly certainly the genus evolved from a rather unspecialized group of five-toed hoofed herbivores belonging to the order Condylarthra. It is probable that this order was also ancestral to the horse-like litopterns of Tertiary South America that became extinct when the establishment of the Central American land bridge allowed a faunal influx from the north. The litopterns were then ousted from their ecological niche by the true horses, the descendants of *Eohippus*.

Fourteen Perissodactyl families of similar origin existed during the Eocene, making the Perissodactyls the dominant herbivores of the epoch. Then, perhaps because of competition from the even more successful Artiodactyls, the order steadily declined in importance, leaving only the horses, the tapirs and the rhinoceroses with us today (figure 1).

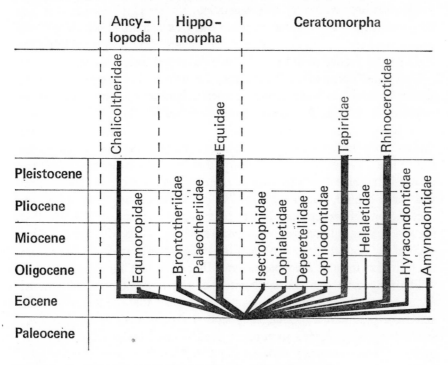

Figure 1. A phylogeny of the Perissodactyls. (After Romer.)

Before continuing with the story of the family Equidae, a brief reference must be made to the other two families of the suborder Hippomorpha, the palaeotheres that, at a time when the American-Eurasian land bridge was broken, carried on an exuberant but short-lived line of horse-like animals in Europe; and the brontotheres or titanotheres that evolved a very unhorse-like group in North America during much the same period.

The paleotheres evolved forms that tended to be large, such as the three-toed *Palaeotherium*, which was the size of a rhinoceros; and others that, though smaller, had some interesting structural developments that seem well in advance of their time: for example, *Plagiolophus* was adapted for plains-living and grazing millions of years before the horses achieved this specialization. Perhaps because of their over-early specialization the palaeotheres died out by the early Oligocene.

Again in the titanotheres the trend was towards giantism, the huge double-horned *Brontotherium* reaching a height of eight feet. But in contrast to the palaeotheres they were strangely unprogressive, retaining the same number of toes as *Eohippus* as well as a similar dentition that could deal only with very soft vegetation. Romer [49] suggests that lack of good teeth was a factor in their early extinction. Their huge bulk required a vast food intake and any slight change in the availability of the right sort of fodder would readily have destroyed their hold on existence.

From the Eocene to the Pleistocene, the main evolutionary centre of the family Equidae was North America whence from time to time some species migrated to Eurasia, Africa and South America.

In sharp distinction to the palaeotheres and titanotheres, the equids evolved in a rather steady and conservative fashion. For instance, the immediate descendants of *Eohippus*, that is *Orohippus* and *Epihippus*, retained the same foot structure as their ancestor with four toes in front and three behind, and a very similar low crowned dentition suited for chewing on soft vegetation. It was only in the late Eocene that the first marked anatomical changes occurred. These had to do with the development of the central nervous system, the brain structure moving away from the primitive form of *Eohippus* towards that of an intelligent mammal.

The Oligocene saw the appearance of the larger three-toed equids, *Mesohippus* and *Miohippus*. Simpson [53] suggests that the loss of one toe may have produced a mechanically stouter arrangement of the foot that would have been needed to support the increased body-weight of these animals. The three-toed foot was still padded but took most of the weight on the middle toe. There were also some marked changes in the teeth, the

8

premolars becoming more like molars. But with all the modifications of structure, *Mesohippus* and *Miohippus* were creatures of the forest and swamp, feeding on leaves and soft vegetation.

In the Miocene came a division into groups that evolved along different lines. One group of three-toed equids continued the ancestral browsing forest-dwelling pattern of life until their extinction in the Pliocene. Other groups that adapted to grazing and a life on the open plain also failed to survive beyond the Pliocene. But one side branch of these three-toed grazers gave rise to one-toed grazing animals that finally developed into the genus *Equus* of the present day.

Among the browsing equids of the Miocene was the pony-sized three-toed *Anchitherium*, which migrated to Eurasia, the first true horse to live in those parts since the Eocene, and reached as far as China. The anchitheres persisted into the Pliocene, including some larger forms often classified separately as *Hyohippus*, and a giant North American form, *Megahippus*. There was also a series of tiny North American browsing horses of the Miocene called *Archaeohippus*.

The transitional form between the browsers and the grazers was *Parahippus* of the North American Miocene, an altogether more horse-like creature than its ancestors, particularly about the head and in the development of the molar teeth. Stirton [55] gives the opinion that *Parahippus* marks one of the most important steps in the evolution of the late Tertiary horses, since it was in this genus and at this time that the inception took place of high-crowned teeth that could withstand a life-time of chewing on tough abrasive grasses as opposed to the soft vegetation that had of necessity been the staple diet of the horses until then. The three-toed foot was retained by this genus but with reduced side-toes that no longer had contact with the ground except presumably at fast paces.

The more advanced species of *Parahippus* are almost indistinguishable from the North-American Miocene genus *Merychippus* which, with its many varieties including *Protohippus*, in its turn intergrades with the equids of the Pliocene, namely *Pliohippus*, *Calippus*, *Hannippus*, *Hipparion* and *Neohipparion*.

The pony-sized *Hipparion* migrated to Eurasia, where the anchitheres had by then died out, and was probably the first horse to penetrate into Africa where it gave rise to *Stylohipparion* that survived until the Pleistocene.

The other three-toed grazers, that is *Neohipparion*, the slender little *Nannippus* and the pigmy *Calippus* did not migrate from North America: they died out during the Pliocene.

9

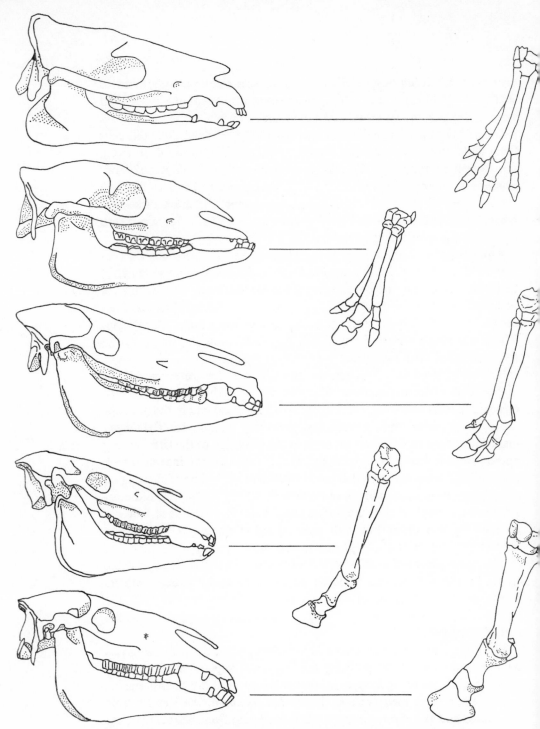

Figure 2. Evolutionary stages in the development of *Equus*. Top to bottom: *Hyracotherium, Mesohippus, Merychippus, Pliohippus, Equus*. (Drawing not to scale: skulls reproduced to same height to show relative proportions.)

Pliohippus continued the trend towards one-toedness with the reduction of the side-toes from semi-functional digits to the apparently functionless splint bones of the modern horses. One group of the genus *Pliohippus* migrated to South America and developed into the sturdy short-legged one-toed *Hippidion* and related genera that became extinct during the Pleistocene. Another group, the subgenus *Astrohippus*, resembled *Equus* both in limb formation and in its dentition, and by the end of the Pliocene graded into that genus.

The early type of *Equus*, the subgenus *Plesippus*, soon migrated to other continents, quickly spreading to Eurasia, Africa and South America. It was about the size of a pony and its teeth had some zebra-like characters, similar to those of *Equus stenonis* of the early Pleistocene of Europe, a species that will be discussed in a later chapter.

Hipparion, which had migrated to Eurasia and Africa during the Pliocene, was still in existence when *Equus* entered those territories some seven million years later. The slender three-toed *Hipparion* did not long survive the new invasion. The European variety died out in the early Pleistocene followed somewhat later by the African species.

The centre of equine evolution shifted during the Pleistocene from the New World to the Old World. It is debatable whether the modern type of *Equus* developed from *Plesippus* in America and emigrated to Eurasia or vice versa. Be as it may, at the end of the Ice Age horses vanished from the American plains that had been their homeland throughout the Tertiary. It will have been noted that the history of Equidae contains a number of examples of such inexplicable extinctions. Kurten [33] points out that in England the horse is missing from the fauna of one of the warm interglacial periods of a hundred thousand years ago: an episode that cannot be attributed to man's activities as there were no men in England at that time.

A summary of what may be called the American period of equine evolution is given in the table overleaf.

Table 2. The Evolution of Equidae, Eocene to Pleistocene

Genus	Epoch	Distribution
Four-toed Browsers		
Hyracotherium (Eohippus)	Eocene	North America and Europe
Orohippus	Eocene	North America
Epihippus	Eocene	North America
Three-toed Browsers		
Mesohippus	Oligocene	North America
Miohippus	Oligocene	North America
Anchitherium	Miocene	North America and Eurasia
Hyohippus	Miocene and early Pliocene	North America and Asia
Megahippus	Pliocene	North America
Archaeohippus	Miocene	North America
Three-toed Intermediate Type		
Parahippus	Miocene	North America
Three-toed Grazers		
Merychippus (Protohippus)	Miocene	North America
Hipparion	Pliocene to early Pleistocene	North America, Eurasia and Africa
Stylohipparion	Pliocene and Pleistocene	Africa
Neohipparion	Pliocene	North America
Nannippus	Pliocene	North America
Calippus	Pliocene	North America
One-toed Grazers		
Pliohippus (Some varieties had slender side-toes)	Pliocene	North America
Hippidion	Pleistocene	South America
Onohippidium	Pleistocene	South America
Hyperhippidium	Pleistocene	South America
Equus	Late Pliocene and Pleistocene	North and South America, Eurasia and Africa

Chapter 3

The Making of *Equus*

Eohippus was unlike *Equus* in many respects. It had a different sort of brain, different dentition, different limbs and feet and a different body shape, size and weight. The transformation from *Eohippus* to *Equus* took fifty million years to effect, a very gradual process to say the least, but the rate of change varied. For instance the rapid evolution of the brain during the Eocene was not matched by similar improvements in the dentition that started only a rapid trend towards high-crowned teeth in the Miocene; and the final change from the multi-digit foot to the single toe of the modern horse did not occur until the Pliocene and then only in one genus, namely *Pliohippus*.

Seven genera of Equidae lead directly to *Pliohippus*. The Eocene genera are barely distinguishable from one another: *Eohippus*, *Orohippus* and *Epihippus* were small forest-dwelling animals with a height at the withers of ten to twenty inches, that is two and a half to five hands (four inches = one hand). The back was arched and flexible, the hind quarters higher than the fore and terminating in a stout tail. The limbs were fairly long and capable of lateral movement as the two bones of the forearm, the radius and ulna, were separate; similarly the tibia and fibula in the hind limb.

There were four toes on the fore-feet and three on the hind, each toe terminating in a small hoof and supported behind by a dog-type pad. The skull was rather short with the orbit set in the middle of its length and without the posterior bar of bone that protects the eye of the later equids. The mouth contained forty-four teeth, namely twelve incisors, four canines, sixteen premolars and twelve molars; and between the premolars and the incisors there is just the beginning of a gap, the diastema or bar of later horses. All the teeth were very low-crowned but the molars show a tendency to form lophs or crests to produce a more efficient grinding surface.

The Oligocene genera, *Mesohippus* and *Miohippus*, were four and a half to seven hands in height and had only three toes on their fore-feet. Except for the first small premolar, all the grinding teeth were now of the same molar pattern with loph formation, though still low-crowned. The diastema had become more marked.

The Miocene genera, *Parahippus* and *Merychippus*, apart from being three-toed, were very like modern ponies of up to about ten and a half hands. The skull was elongated and the back of the eye was protected by the beginning of the post-orbital bar of bone, which became complete in later genera. The radius was fused with the ulna, and the tibia with the fibula, thus limiting lateral movements of the limbs and confining them fairly strictly to a fore and aft pendulum action. And, the most important change of all, the teeth had become definitely high-crowned, and patterned like those of a modern horse, giving a hard-wearing chewing apparatus that broke the old dependence on soft foliage and allowed the Equidae to feed on the coarse tough grasses of the prairies and steppes that spread across the American and Eurasian landscapes during the Miocene.

Pliohippus was even more horse-like than its immediate predecessors and with their single toes its advanced species were almost identical with the early forms of Equus. However in general *Equus* was a larger animal, with higher, larger and more complicated teeth.

The increasing size and weight of the successive genera leading through *Pliohippus* to *Equus* may well have necessitated a change in the locomotor apparatus. Simpson has pointed out that enlarging an animal to four times its original height without change of proportions would make it sixty-four times as heavy, while the absolute strength of bone and muscle would be only sixteen times greater. Such an animal would be so unsound mechanically that it could scarcely move without risk of fracturing bones or spraining muscles and tendons. The bodily proportions and limbs of the Equidae did in fact alter in a far more fundamental fashion than is often imagined: it was not just a matter of a reduction in the number of toes.

Eohippus walked on its pads like a dog and used its hooves, which were little more than blunt claws, only for thrusting off at a run. When galloping its flexible spine would have given extra length to its stride.

Equus on the other hand has a fairly rigid spine, the bones of the upper parts of the limbs are short, powerful and well-muscled, the lower parts of the limbs are relatively long, slender and unmuscled, and the animal stands poised on its hooves which incorporate the ancestral foot-pad in the form of the frog. At a gallop, the horse thrusts off from the ground with its hind

Figure 3. The horse in motion: the full phase of the gallop.

limbs and swings the body forward by pivoting over the fore-limbs. The jar passed to the limbs at every stride by such a comparatively heavy animal when moving at high speeds is minimized by a beautifully co-ordinated shock-absorbing arrangement of flexible joints, ligaments and tendons. And the elastic recoil of some of these structures, particularly the suspensory ligament and the inferior sesamoidean ligaments, flicks back the foot immediately after it strikes the ground, producing an automatic springing action which, aided by the slightly slower response of the flexor muscles and tendons, catapults the animal forward.

Associated with this spring mechanism is the ingenious 'stay apparatus' that automatically supports the body when at rest and enables the horse to relax and to sleep while standing without undue muscular fatigue or risk that its legs may give way.

The spring-support mechanism was elaborated in the course of the evolution of the Equidae, apparently to compensate for the loss of the support and resilience of the multi-digit foot and its pads and to bear the increasing body weight. For instance *Mesohippus* is the first genus to show signs of the strengthening and increase in number of the inferior sesa-moidean ligaments; and the suspensory ligament, which nowadays seldom contains any muscle tissue whatsoever, was developed during the Miocene from the interosseous muscle that helped in the flexing of the limbs of the earlier horses.

In fact the history of this mechanism appears to have involved the strengthening of the points where the greatest stresses occur, particularly in the fore limb which carries more than half the weight of the body. In a detailed exposition of the evolution of the digital ligaments of the horse, Camp and Smith [10] remark that the development of such a complex ligamentary system has evidently exacted a penalty. Among fossil as well as domesticated horses no part of the body is so liable to become injured and permanently disabled, or to develop periosteal exostes. To this one must add that the average height of the English thoroughbred has in-

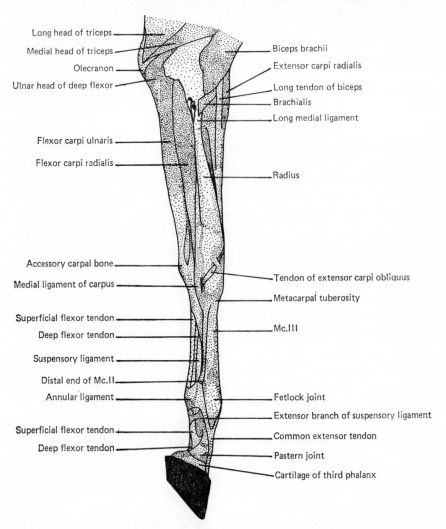

Figure 4. Tendons and ligaments of the horse's leg. (After Sisson and Grossman.)

creased six inches in the past two hundred years and a fair proportion of lameness and leg troubles may be attributable to some breeds of the domestic horse having been pushed to their mechanical limits in the efforts to produce bigger and faster animals.

The lengthening and other adaptations of the limb for speed introduced a number of weaknesses besides those just mentioned. The long flexor tendons, stretching from above the knee and hock to the phalanges, are very prone to sprains and other injuries; the rudimentary third and fourth metacarpals, the splint bones, are a frequent source of trouble; and the numerous pathological conditions to which the bones and other structures of the foot are liable, cause a large proportion of the acute and chronic lamenesses that afflict the domestic horse.

On the other hand the Equidae evolved a dentition that, compared with man's, is remarkably trouble-free, perhaps because the whole design was based on the provision of very hard-wearing grinding teeth. Of the forty-four teeth of *Eohippus* only four, the first premolars, were discarded during the evolution to *Equus* and even these may be found in a vestigial form in the upper jaw of the modern horse: the so-called wolf-teeth or eye-teeth, which erupt between five or six months of age and often fall out naturally when the permanent premolars appear; in former times they were thought to cause defective vision and were extracted for that reason. In the lower jaw similar vestiges of the first premolars may be present but they rarely erupt through the gum. The other premolars were converted to a molar-like form during the Eocene, giving, with the true molars, twenty-four low-crowned or brachydont grinding teeth, made up of two hard substances, dentine and enamel.

During the Miocene, the *Parahippus* line started the trend towards high-crowned or hypsodont teeth, that is large prism-shaped teeth deeply embedded in the jaw-bone from which, as the exposed part is worn away, they thrust up to maintain a functional crown of about four-fifths of an inch in height. An essential feature of this development is the hard cement, which in early equids was confined to the roots of the teeth, and now comes to cover the molars and to fill in the interstices between the dentine and the enamel on their crowns. The three materials wear at different rates and so produce an excellent rough grinding surface. A disadvantage of the system is that the tables of the upper and lower molars work slant-wise over each other, an action that in time wears sharp jagged edges to the teeth that may cut the insides of the cheeks and make feeding a slow and painful process.

The size and shape of the teeth and the molar patterns of the various genera of the Equidae are quite distinctive and if other parts of the skeleton are missing, it is possible to identify a fossil genus on the evidence of one tooth alone; and luckily teeth are the most plentiful and best preserved of fossils. And the age of a horse may be gauged fairly accurately from a study of the amount of wear on the tables of the incisor teeth and from the angle at which they are set in the mouth; this varies from upright in young animals to very sloping in the aged. One is helped by a knowledge of the periods in life when various teeth erupt and when the milk teeth are replaced by the permanent dentition.

Table of Dentition (after Sisson [54])

Average period of eruption of the teeth of the horse:

Deciduous or milk teeth

first incisor	birth or first week
second incisor	4–6 weeks
third incisor	6–9 months
first premolar	
second premolar	birth or first 3 weeks
third premolar	

Permanent teeth

first incisor	$2\frac{1}{2}$ years
second incisor	$3\frac{1}{2}$ years
third incisor	$4\frac{1}{2}$ years
first premolar (wolf-tooth)	5–6 months
second premolar	$2\frac{1}{2}$ years
third premolar	3 years
fourth premolar	4 years
first molar	9–12 months
second molar	2 years
third molar	$3\frac{1}{2}$–4 years

Contemporary with the evolution of the large, hypsodont, heavily cemented teeth of the Miocene equids was the development of the typical long-muzzled equine head and its strong supporting neck muscles. Edinger [17] has shown, interestingly enough, that the elongation of the facial skull and the enlargement of the teeth were associated with a spectacular enlargement of the anterior pituitary lobe. Indeed the whole pituitary gland increased its volume four or five-fold during the period of transition from *Mesohippus* to *Equus*. However the most vigorous phase in the evolution of the brain itself took place still further back, in the Eocene, before any major changes had occurred in bones, teeth or body size.

The brain of *Eohippus* was of a very primitive and unspecialized type, in striking contrast to the quite advanced structure of the rest of the body. It was not until *Orohippus* that equids acquired a brain that was definitely that of a higher mammal, with marked expansion of cerebrum that in *Mesohippus* and later genera became increasingly prominent. In a careful study of endocranial casts of fossils Equidae Edinger [11] showed that throughout the evolution of the equine brain each of its divisions increased in absolute size but at different rates. The type of brain characterizing ungulates today was not achieved before the late Miocene and in its development progress was not in every phase linked with either increase in body size or skeletal specialization. By the Pliocene the Equidae had modern, if small, horse brains and the brain of the Pleistocene *Equus* was almost identical with that of a modern horse of the same size.

Chapter 4

The Horses of the Ice Age

AT the beginning of the Pleistocene, when the general climate of the world was becoming cooler but long before the great glacial periods, there were two major migrations of *Equus* from North America, one southwards and one eastwards.

The southerly migration across the Isthmus of Panama into the South American continent seems to have crowded out the earlier equid migrants, the descendants of *Pliohippus*, which had flourished in their new habitat and evolved into short-legged heavy-headed animals of the genera *Hippidion, Onohippidium* and *Parahippidium*. A peculiar feature of these genera is the great length and slenderness of the nasal bones, which has given rise to the suggestion that they may have possessed short trunks.

The eastward migration across the Bering land bridge into Eurasia similarly displaced the *Hipparion* from its ecological niche in the Old World where, for about seven million years, it had been the dominant faunal element and the sole representative of the Equidae: the Eurasian species became extinct almost immediately after the arrival of *Equus*, to be followed into oblivion some time later, in the middle Pleistocene, by the African species.

The *Hipparions* were, in their epoch, a highly successful group that migrated from North America in the early Pliocene and colonized much of Asia, Europe and North Africa. Usually they were to be found with the plains-dwelling animals, such as the antelopes, but several species adapted to a woodland environment. In general the *Hipparions* resembled small lightly built horses and in Spain a graceful little gazelle-like species existed. Another small species, found in Greece, was once proposed as a possible ancestor of the *Equus* of the Old World; a contention that is supported neither by the sequence of the fossil record nor by a comparison of the skeletons and teeth of the two genera.

20

Hipparion can be distinguished from *Equus* by the three-toed foot, by the typical pattern of the enamel on the surface of the molar teeth and by a deep pit or fossa in the skull below the orbit. This fossa, which supposedly lodged a scent-gland similar to the larmier of deer, first appeared among the Equidae in *Merychippus* and it recurs in a number of its descendants. But in *Equus* it is either absent or very shallow; and that area of the skull merely serves as a point of origin for the *levator labii superioris proprius*, the muscle that raises the upper lips. Nevertheless from time to time it has been suggested that the preorbital depression occasionally seen in the horse indicates a link with *Hipparion*. For instance Lydekker [38] in a paper he read before the Zoological Society of London in 1904, described 'a vestige of the Hipparion's face-pit' in the skull of an Indian domesticated horse in the collection of the British Museum and spoke of a similar depression in the skulls of some Arab horses and English thoroughbreds, including that of the famous racehorse Bend Or; in a later publication [39] Lydekker more or less recanted but the controversy attracted a lot of public interest at that period and his original views are still quoted now and again by enthusiastic holders of the belief that the Arab is of different lineage from other breeds of horse.

The early migrant species of *Equus* dispersed widely across the Old World: the fairly large *E. sivalensis* and *E. sanmeniensis* had their habitat respectively in India and China by the early Pleistocene; at a later date the rather smaller *E. stenonis* appeared in Europe. All these animals had a zebra-like dentition and into the bargain may have been striped like zebras. *E. stenonis* gave rise to at least one other zebrine form, namely *E. sussenborensis*, which survived in Germany until the first great glaciation. Thereafter the zebras disappeared from Eurasia and became purely African species.

The *stenonis* group included a variety of forms and it is usually considered to have given rise not only to other zebrine animals but also to the caballine horses, the forebears of the domestic *E. caballus*, and to the asinine horses. Kurten [33] states that the first member of genus *Equus* to enter Europe was a huge caballine animal, *E. bressanus*, preceding the advent there of *stenonis*, its supposed ancestral group. Later *stenonis* and *bressanus* inhabited the same European localities.

On the other hand Hopwood [30] casts doubts on the probability of the caballine horses having been derived from *stenonis* when the two groups were obviously contemporaries. Instead he suggests that they evolved independently, perhaps in North America rather than in Eurasia, from the animals grouped generically under *Pliohippus* and *Plesippus*. He is sure that 'the zebrine group is the older and more primitive, the first wave of a migration from an unknown source'.

E. bressanus, also called the *robustus* horse, is described by Kurten as being of enormous size, rivalling that of the biggest living cart-horses. Its descendants, *E. mosbachensis*, *E. germanicus* and others were of lesser stature but still sturdy animals and it is understandable that in the past they have been proposed as the direct ancestors of the domestic breeds of heavy horses. However relatively suddenly during the period of the last great glaciation they were replaced by the modern species *E. przewalskii*, which became very abundant throughout Eurasia and eventually, some thousands of years after the Ice Age had ended, man learned to domesticate and to depend upon for transport and haulage in both peace and war.

But to Stone-Age man wild horses were just another form of game, though a very important one, along with mammoth, reindeer and other animals that inhabited the tundras and steppes bordering the ice-covered regions. During the Middle and Late Palaeolithic times, man made increasing use of caves, presumably to escape from the intense cold, and these dwellings often contain vast numbers of animal bones to bear witness to his success as a hunter. Notable examples are to be found in the caves of the limestone regions of Western Europe, such as those at Solutré, near Mâcon in south-eastern France, where Pietrémont [46] has described an astonishing collection of the bones of thousands of horses of the *przewalski* type, to which he gave the name '*le magma de cheval*'.

A constant feature of such accumulations of the fossil remains of horses is that they contain few vertebrae or ribs but are made up almost entirely of the limb bones of adults, which have been split open to obtain the marrow, and skulls, which have been cracked open to extract the brain. It seems that the hunters usually selected mature animals as their quarry and preferred to dismember them at the site of the kill rather than drag the carcases back to their caves. Sometimes the horses' tails were removed, either as trophies or perhaps because the long tail hairs were used as thread or twisted into string.

Horsemeat was clearly an important human food in Europe at this period and it is curious that one of the staple items of the diet of Stone Age man should have become almost taboo to many of his descendants. Pietrémont [46] attributes the abolition of the eating of horseflesh in Central Europe to the efforts of the early Christian Church to stamp out various pagan rites supposed to be associated with such feasting. In support of this thesis he quotes two papal letters specifically prohibiting this heathen practice, addressed to Boniface, the apostle of Germany during the eighth century. Similarly Lommel [37] states that the first Borgia pope, Calixtus III (1455-8), a Spaniard and a former archbishop of Valencia, was at pains to forbid the celebration of religious rites in a certain Spanish cave that was decorated with the pictures of horses. The reference to cave pictures at that period of history is of interest because they were not as it were officially discovered until 1879, in the first instance at Altamira in Spain, although it is common to find that long before this there were ancient local legends associating the localities of rock paintings with hauntings and animal apparitions.

It is likely that the Ice Age paintings and drawings of the horse and other beasts of the chase did in fact have a great deal more than a purely decorative value for Palaeolithic man. The animals are often shown with arrows flying into them and frequently the pictures contain abstract slatted signs that might represent traps designed to hold either the body or the spirit of the animal. In other words the rock paintings were a form of sympathetic magic created to bring success to the tribal hunting groups and perhaps also to propitiate the spirits of the slain animals.

The cave art of France and Spain dates back some thirty thousand years, starting with crude engravings and simple outlines of animals and culminating in the bold naturalistic paintings of the Magdalenian period of 15,000 to 10,000 BC, splendidly exemplified at Lascaux, Font de Gaume, Altamira and elsewhere.

The horses depicted are very similar in make, shape and upright mane to *E. przewalskii*, which accords well with the fossil record. However at Pech-Merle there is a picture, dated at around 20,000 BC, that shows horses with large spots on their bodies and on the background. The spots are thought to have been put there in the belief that they would increase the fecundity of the wild-horse herds and not to indicate any natural body markings. And perhaps not too much notice should be taken of the colouring of the pictures as the choice of pigments was limited mainly to black oxide of manganese and the red and yellow oxides of iron.

The end of the Ice Age in Europe came comparatively rapidly between 9000 and 8000 BC. The retreat of the great glaciers that had covered Scandinavia, Britain and much of northern Europe allowed new types of vegetation to spread across the previously barren waste, and forests replaced the treeless periglacial tundra. Reindeer and some other arctic species followed the ice northward; many kinds of animal simply died out,

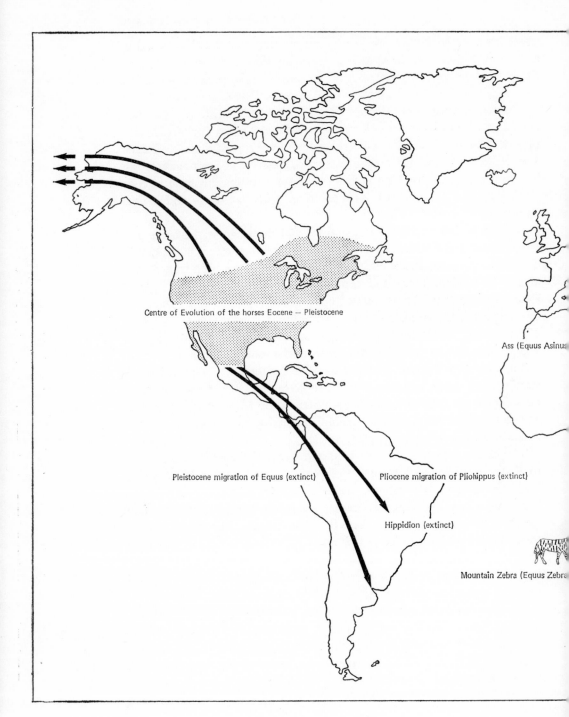

Figure 5. Geographic distribution of equine species.

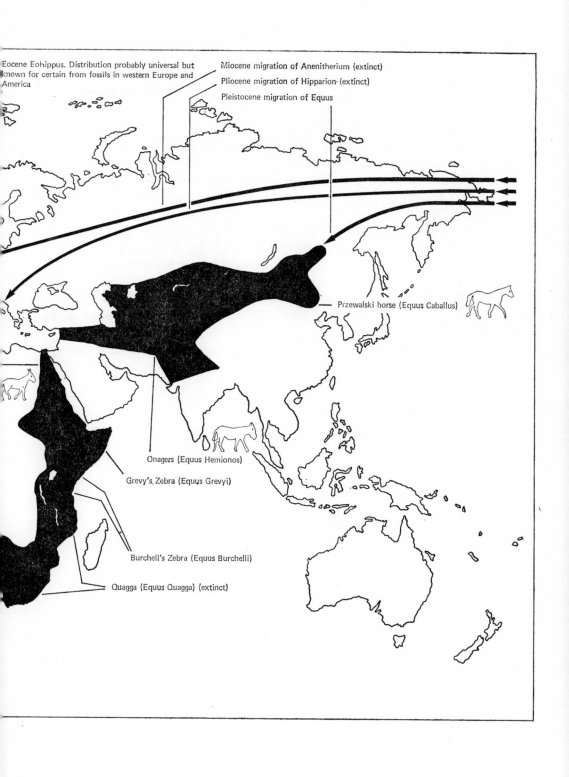

Eocene Eohippus. Distribution probably universal but known for certain from fossils in western Europe and America

Miocene migration of Anenitherium (extinct)

Pliocene migration of Hipparion (extinct)

Pleistocene migration of Equus

Przewalski horse (Equus Caballus)

Onagers (Equus Hemionos)

Grevy's Zebra (Equus Grevyi)

Burchell's Zebra (Equus Burchelli)

Quagga (Equus Quagga) (extinct)

both in Eurasia and in the Americas, where *Equus* was among the species that suffered extinction; the rain belts also shifted northwards, leaving parts of northern Africa and southwestern Asia to become arid deserts and causing further disturbance of animal life. The human hunters would have been impelled to follow the migration of the animals to the new feeding grounds but game was less plentiful than before and more widely dispersed: hunting became a very precarious source of livelihood in many areas. It was in this dramatically changed world that man turned to agriculture and to the domestication of food-producing animals, namely sheep, goats, cattle and pigs.

The domestication of the horse came some five thousand years later, and during the period between the end of the Ice Age and about 3000 BC horses were just a natural part of the wild fauna of Europe and Asia, with the wide steppes of the centre of the Eurasian continent as their most favoured habitat. The other members of the genus *Equus* were arranged in fairly well-defined geographical areas: the onagers and kiangs mostly in the deserts and mountainous regions of Asia, Syria and Arabia; the asses in northern and northeastern Africa and the zebras in southern and eastern Africa.

Chapter 5

Wild Horses

AT one time wild horses were abundant on the Eurasian steppes and as typical of that environment as zebras on the savannahs of Africa. Then, at around 3000 BC, the steppe peoples adopted the nomadic way of life and, one may imagine, discovered in their wide wanderings with their herds that horses were more useful to them alive as a means of transporting their belongings than dead as a source of food. It is likely that to some of the peoples their horse herds were almost their sole livelihood, providing not only transport but also milk and meat as well as skins, which could be used for clothing or made into tents – Tartar tribes have lived in this manner into recent times.

The innovation of horse transport increased the mobility of the nomads and eased their travels over the vast distances of the steppes that extend, with few natural obstacles, across eastern Europe and western Asia from the Carpathians to the Pamirs, and beyond into Mongolia and China. Movement to the north was limited by adverse climatic conditions and westward migration was obstructed by the deep forests of central Europe, but apart from these factors it was inevitable that the nomads should be attracted, whether for trade, settlement, sporadic raids or for actual invasion, to the rich emergent civilizations of the Near and Middle East and China, where the value of the domesticated horse was immediately appreciated, chiefly because it enabled a potent new military weapon to be developed – the swift war-chariot – and so an insatiable demand for horses was created at a time when the ways and means of breeding them in large numbers were little understood.

The capture of their young for domestication, the competition with domesticated animals for grazing and for watering places, coupled with the effects of being over-hunted as game, depleted the wild herds and drove them into regions remote from man. Even in Roman times, reports of the existence in Europe of wild horses were somewhat suspect as such animals could have been merely the descendants of domesticated horses that had run wild; and much the same could be said of similar stories in later ages. In fact by the nineteenth century most orthodox naturalists tended towards the belief that there had been no truly wild horses since prehistoric times.

The scepticism of the scientific world can well be imagined therefore when, in 1881, the Russian naturalist I. S. Poliakoff proposed a distinct species of wild horse, *Equus przewalskii* Poliakoff, as a result of his examination of the skull and skin of one three-year-old animal presented to the Zoological Museum of St Petersburg by the explorer Colonel N. M. Przewalski. Przewalski had received the specimen as a gift from the chief magistrate of Zaisan, who had obtained it from some hunters of wild camel in the Gobi Desert of western Mongolia. Flower [22] may have summarized the general feeling rather mildly when he wrote: 'Until more specimens are obtained it is difficult to form an opinion as to the validity of the species, or to resist the suspicion that it may not be an accidental hybrid between the kiang and the horse'.

Actually more specimens were obtained by Salensky [50] of the St Petersburg Zoological Museum and his anatomical studies showed that in general the teeth and skeleton of the Przewalski horse resembled those of the domestic horse but that there were some intriguing external differences: 'The species is of extraordinary interest since, in it, the characters of the domestic horse (e.g. the presence of callosities or 'chestnuts' on all four limbs) are mixed with features reminding one of the Asiatic ass (e.g. erect mane and form of tail). These characters, and especially the form of tail, do not agree perfectly with the like feature in the ass but from something intermediate between the characters of the horse and those of the ass.'

And Ridgeway [48] states that Professor J. C. Ewart [18] provided one of the most telling arguments against the hybrid theory with a practical breeding experiment that demonstrated that the offspring resulting from kiang-pony crossings were quite different animals from the Przewalski horse. Moreover the hybrid is sterile while the Przewalski horses are a fertile species among themselves and produce fertile offspring when crossed with domestic horses.

The Przewalski horse is now accepted as the sole surviving race of wild horse of the type from which the domestic horse is descended, and, although it may seem illogical to name the wild form after the domestic form, it is officially designated as a sub-species of *Equus caballus* with the name *Equus caballus przewalskii*.

It is an animal of twelve to fourteen hands in height, with a heavy head and broad muzzle. The usual colour is a yellow dun with a lighter shade on the sides and belly, and a mealy nose. There may be a faint dark reddish-brown stripe along the back and across the shoulders, and sometimes there may be striping near the knees and hocks. Like many moorland ponies it grows a long woolly winter coat and side-whiskers on its face; and its tail, though long, has a fan of short stiff hairs covering its base. In contrast to the domestic horse, the mane is short, stiff and erect; it is shed annually, and there is therefore usually insufficient time for a forelock to develop.

Little is known of the habits of the Przewalski horse in the wild and the only detailed firsthand report seems to be that of the brothers Grum-Grjimailo, who were responsible for the collection of specimens in the Gobi desert for the St Petersburg Zoological Museum. Their account, which is quoted by Salensky [50] and other authors, runs as follows:

The wild horse is an inhabitant of the level districts, and goes at night to the pasture-lands and drinking places. At break of day he returns to the desert, where he rests until sunset. In the spring when there are foals in the herd, the animals always rest in the same place. The fact that I found a place of about 18 square metres covered with a thick layer of foals' dung affords proof of this habit. From the almost entire absence of coarser dung it may be assumed that the resting place of the herd is changed as soon as the foals grow up; whereas it is constantly the same so long as the foals are small.

The wild horses generally walk one behind the other, especially when avoiding a danger. From the habit the horses have of walking in a line behind each other, deeply trodden paths are found in the whole district.

One of the most certain indications of the presence of the wild horse in a district is the occurrence of enormous heaps of dung along the paths. From this characteristic, a herdsman remarked that the horses had gone to the drinking places the day before; and we confirmed the significance of the indication immediately on our arrival at Gashun. In case of danger, the stallion runs forward only if the herd contains no foals; and even then he often runs to the side and shows by his movements an extraordinary disquiet.

The Mongolians have made many efforts to tame the wild horse but in vain; the horse will not submit to man, is afraid of him and cannot be rendered serviceable. The capture of the wild horse, as practised by the Mongolians, is a very simple affair. At the time when the mares foal, the Kalmuks betake themselves to the plains with two horses. Having discovered the herd, they follow it until such a time as the still weak foals can go no further. The foals are then taken away and reared in a herd of domestic horses.

In general the behaviour of Przewalski horses bred and reared in captivity does not differ much from that of members of the domestic species
whose natural responses have not been inhibited by special training and
handling. There is a similar use of the voice: neighing and nickering as a
form of greeting and intercommunication, and in the expectancy of finding
food or water; squealing as a threat or warning and as an indication of
anger and frustration; the same use of the ears, tail and head-carriage
to indicate the various moods; and of hooves and teeth for defence and
aggression. Mohr [42] states that Przewalski mares carry their young from
320 to 343 days, which is within the normal duration of pregnancy in the
domestic animal; and that, in Prague, the majority of foals are born in
May, with a fair number at the end of April and in June to the beginning
of July, the births generally occurring at night. The normal weight at
birth is around fifty-five to sixty-five pounds and by morning the foal is
strong and active.

It is just possible that a small wild herd of Przewalski horses may still
survive in the area of the Takhin Shar-nuru massif, 'The Mountain of the
Yellow Horses', in south-western Mongolia, close to the Chinese frontier.
The species is known to have existed in this region for hundreds of years
but its original ancestral habitat must have been elsewhere: in the narrative
of the Central Asiatic Expedition in Mongolia and China, 1921–30 [3], it is
stated that one of the most remarkable features of the Cenozoic fauna of
the Gobi is the complete absence of the Equidae, though in the fossil record
of northern China itself *Hipparion* and *Equus* are well represented.

The species is under strict State protection on both sides of the border
and severe penalties would be imposed for any breach of the law but no
sign of the animals has been seen for several years and the continuance of
the species almost certainly now depends on the maintenance of breeding
nuclei in zoos and special reserves; of particular importance in this respect
is the herd at the Prague Zoo where *The International Studbook of the
Przewalski Horse* is maintained.

Przewalski's horse is also sometimes referred to as the Mongolian tarpan:
tarpan being a common colloquial term for a wild horse. Mohr [42] relates
that Przewalski himself described one of his specimens as a new variety of
tarpan, only to be corrected by Poliakoff who said it was entirely different
from the tarpans seen in the Black Sea and Caspian regions by earlier
travellers such as Gmelin, who in his travels through Russia during 1733
to 1743 noted the existence of numerous wild herds of small mouse-coloured
horses with short curly manes.

These southern Russian tarpans were small sturdy ponies easily distinguishable from the Przewalski horse. Even in their heyday, during the seventeenth and eighteenth centuries, tarpans probably carried a considerable admixture of domestic blood: owing among other things to the notorious proneness of tarpan stallions to drive domestic mares into their harems whenever opportunity offered. The last wild tarpans became extinct in the middle of the nineteenth century; the last captive specimen died in 1919.

The name tarpan is still used for domestic horses leading a feral existence in parts of eastern Europe, as well as for the so-called 'reconstructed tarpans', which are the result of mating Przewalski stallions to Polish Konik ponies: the offspring are stated to possess all the physical characteristics of the extinct southern Russian tarpan and, after a number of generations of selection, to breed true to this type.

Chapter 6

Asiatic Wild Asses

AT a distance, in its native deserts, the half-ass, *Equus hemionus*, has often been mistaken for the Przewalski horse with which it has many characteristics in common; equally it is similar in some respects to the true wild ass, though that animal is confined to the African continent while the range of hemionus is the arid tract of Asia stretching from Mongolia to Arabia.

The Asiatic wild ass is a rangy, lightly built animal of up to thirteen hands in height; if some allowance is made for the difference in the shading of the winter and summer coats, it can be said that the upper parts of the body are sandy-coloured, while the lower parts, limbs and muzzle are near-white; down the spine there is a dark stripe; the mane is short, erect and without a forelock; the tail is short-haired and ends in a dark tuft; the hoofs are broad and horse-like; the ears are intermediate in size between those of the horse and the ass, and like the ass and the zebra the half-ass has the horny callosities known as the chestnuts on the fore-limbs only.

The chestnuts, or night-eyes, as they are sometimes called in America, are oval horny growths about two inches long found on the inside of the fore-limb, above the knee, in all the species of the Equidae, and on the lower part of the hock in most but not all horses. They are however invariably missing from the hind-limbs of the half-asses, asses and zebras. Because they are apparently functionless it is generally supposed, perhaps illogically, that they must be vestigial remains of once functional organs: for instance, scent-glands such as those found on the limbs of some species of deer, or a more commonly held theory is that they represent the foot-pads of the now vanished first digit of the Equidae of the Eocene epoch. Another horny growth, the ergot, is found in the tuft of hair at the back of the fetlock. The ergots are usually regarded as the vestiges of the pads of the second and fourth digits, and to some extent they may still serve their supposed ancient function by protecting the back of the fetlock when

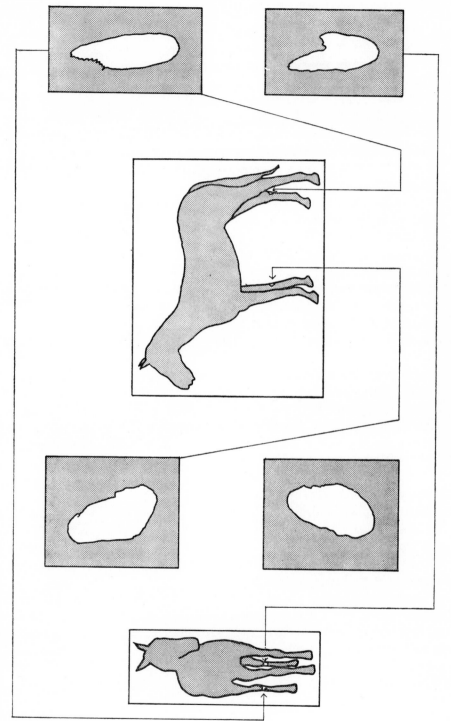

Figure 6. 'Chestnuts' of horse's limb.

at full gallop that joint is over-extended and comes in contact with the ground.

Five races of the Asiatic wild ass are recognized, distinguished from one another by slight differences in size and colour. These are namely the Mongolian kulan, *Equus hemionus hemionus*; the Tibetan kiang, *Equus hemionus kiang*; the Persian onager, *Equus hemionus onager*; the Indian ghor-khar, *Equus hemionus khur*; and the Syrian wild ass, *Equus hemionus hemippus*, which is now almost certainly extinct despite rumours of its survival in South Arabia and Oman which Fisher *et al.* [21] think refer merely to the sighting of feral donkeys.

All races of the Asiatic wild ass prefer the unrestricted views and wide expanses of the open country where their alertness and speed give them the maximum protection from their enemies the wolves. Although typical desert animals in this respect, they do need to drink every two to three days and during the dry season they tend to stay within fairly easy reach of water; only in winter when snow or surface water is on the ground, or in spring when lush vegetation is plentiful, are they free to wander great distances from the water-holes and streams. They are reputed to be strong swimmers and the kiangs positively revel in the icy rivers and lakes of their native highlands.

Their speed and endurance are proverbial, also their curiosity. Lydekker [38] describes how on the plateaux of Ladek and Tibet small troops of kiang would gallop round and round a mounted traveller and how young kiang were in the habit of walking almost into a camp from sheer inquisitiveness. As to their speed and endurance, it used to be said that hunters required a whole relay of horses to capture one of these wild asses; and, more recently, Allen [1] has described how kulan will race alongside a car at speeds of around forty miles an hour. One animal when pursued by a car on the open plain was run down only after a chase of twenty-nine miles, for sixteen miles of which the average speed was thirty miles an hour. He also mentions the kulan's liking for grazing in company with the desert-living gazelle and tells of one stallion that had a particular gazelle as his constant companion day and night.

The mares carry their young for much the same period as the true asses and the zebras, that is about twelve months. Soon after birth the foals are on their feet and very early in life they are sufficiently active to be capable of outrunning a wolf, so it is said, and of travelling up to twenty miles in a day.

The beginning of the foaling and mating season usually sees the small

34

troops of hemionus coming together to form large herds. There is constant fighting between the males for sexual dominance and the hard-bitten scarred appearance of older stallions testifies to the viciousness of the contests that drive the weaker ones out of the herd to lead a solitary existence; and during this period the normally rather silent animals make frequent use of their voice, which has in it elements of both the neigh of the horse and the bray of a donkey, described as a sort of shrieking bray, for challenge and defiance. 1912695

It seems that in Mesopotamia at any rate the onager was domesticated long before the horse. Zeuner [67] states that the ancient Sumerians used them for drawing carts in a similar manner to oxen, with a nose-ring as the means of control; and in Roman times onager foals were captured for use as stud animals in the production of riding mules of better quality and with an easier gait than the more common donkey-horse hybrid. However, there is no doubt that the onager took less kindly to domesticity than did the horse, which rapidly replaced it as the main source of animal traction in the ancient world.

In more recent times hemionus has been mostly sought after for its flesh, which compares with the noblest venison and is credited with various medicinal and aphrodisiac properties, and despite State protection it is still hunted to this day. But the main cause of its continued rapid decline in numbers is the steady encroachment of domestic livestock on the tradi- tional feeding grounds and water-holes, thus driving these wild animals, which through constant harassment have become averse to the slightest contact with man, into remoter regions where they can exist undisturbed – at least for a while.

Fisher et al. [21] state that the kiang of Tibet is now rare but in no immediate danger of extinction; that the ghor-khar, which formerly ranged widely in dry north-western India and West Pakistan, is reduced to under a thousand individuals, mostly in the Little Rann of Kutch, and a few in southern Sind; that about seven hundred onager are maintained under stringent protection on the Badkhyz Reserve of the USSR, while a like number probably still exist in the salt steppes of Iran; and the kulan, once plentiful in Mongolia, Siberia, Manchuria, Chinese Turkestan and in parts of European Russia, is now restricted to the more inaccessible desert regions of Mongolia, where it may number several thousands.

Chapter 7

African Wild Asses and Donkeys

THE European wild ass, *Equus hydruntinus*, was one of the many types of animal that failed to survive the vast changes that followed the break-up of the great glaciers of the Ice Age. It was a slenderly built animal, similar in size and outward appearance to *Equus hemionus* but differing from hemionus in having donkey-like teeth. Rare at the beginning of the Pleistocene, *Equus hydruntinus* became common enough later on and Kurten states that the fossil beds of the late Pleistocene provide ample evidence of the presence of the ass in all parts of Europe at that time. However at the end of the Ice Age the species disappeared completely, leaving none of its stock to contribute to the ancestry of the modern ass, *Equus asinus*, in either its wild or domestic forms.

Equus asinus has inhabited the African continent since the Pleistocene. Domestic forms have been found in the remains of Neolithic settlements of the Near East and the art of ancient Egypt shows that the donkey was known and used in that country as a pack animal long before the horse was brought into the service of man.

Three races of wild ass are thought to have contributed to the domestic donkey stock. One, the Algerian ass, *Equus asinus atlanticus*, has been extinct since Roman times; the other two, the Nubian ass and the Somali ass, have become very rare but may still survive in the remoter desert regions of north-eastern Africa.

The Nubian wild ass, *Equus asinus africanus*, is a mouse-coloured animal with a whitish muzzle and belly. Typically there is a short dark stripe over the withers, at right angles to the narrow dorsal stripe; this characteristic cross over the shoulders is often seen in the domestic donkey and there is a pleasant legend that it commemorates the first Palm Sunday when Our Lord rode into Jerusalem on a donkey. The mane is short and erect; the tail is short-haired for most of its length and ends in a long tuft of hair; the ears are large, the hoofs are smaller and narrower than those of the horse and hemionus; the gestation period is twelve months. The voice is the familiar nerve-shattering bray of the domestic donkey but otherwise the nature of the wild and domestic varieties is very different. In *The Red Book* [21] Sir Samuel Baker is quoted as saying:

Those who have seen donkeys only in their civilised state have no conception of the beauty of the wild or original animal. It is the perfection of activity and courage, and has a high-bred tone in its deportment, a high-actioned step when it trots freely over the rocks and sand, with the speed of a horse when it gallops freely over the boundless desert. No animal is more difficult to approach; and although they are frequently captured by the Arabs those taken are invariably foals, which are ridden down by fast dromedaries, while the mothers escape.

Formerly the Nubian wild ass was found in the stony hills and desert areas of Nubia and other parts of north-eastern Africa but Fisher *et al.* [21] fear that there are now few if any truly wild herds in existence. Though they add that an interesting group of Nubian-type asses is to be found running wild on the Indian Ocean island of Socotra, reputedly the descendants of stock originally brought to the island by ancient Egyptian incense collectors. A small herd of wild asses has also found a safe sanctuary on the northern edge of the Great Libyan Sand Sea, among treacherous salt marshes where it is dangerous and difficult for man to follow them.

The Somali wild ass, *Equus asinus somalicus*, lacks the shoulder stripe of the Nubian variety and is further distinguished from it by having a number of thin black horizontal stripes on its legs. Small herds may still be found in the Sudan, Ethiopia and Somalia. The fact that the flesh of the wild ass is a forbidden food to the Muslim inhabitants of those countries is only a slight protection as the fat of the wild ass is highly prized as a specific against tuberculosis and the animal is therefore well worth hunting. However, as usual, the main threat to existence comes from the ever-increasing expansion of the domestic herds of sheep, goats and cattle that monopolize the limited grazing areas of those arid regions and drive out the wild herbivora.

Here in Britain, the domestic donkey is little more than a family pet but it was once, and in some places still is, the hardest-worked and worst treated of all the domestic animals, receiving the bare minimum of food needed to keep it alive for its labours.

Although sometimes used for riding or in the plough and for other forms of haulage, the main function of the donkey has always been that of a patient carrier of heavy loads and because of its ability to exist on a frugal diet and to withstand neglect, it has for centuries been the typical poor man's beast of burden in many parts of the world. Certainly it lacks the prestige enjoyed by the horse but is nevertheless so useful that it has been introduced into countries as distant from its original African home as South America and China; in Britain it does not seem to have been well known until the Saxon era. It has also been kept as a milk producer, especially in medieval times when it was appreciated that because of the low-fat and high-sugar content asses' milk made an excellent easily digested diet for the sick. And Flower [22] mentions that in the nineteenth century there were great herds of donkeys in Africa in a district to the east of the Dinka country, which the natives maintained purely for milking and not as work animals.

Usually the donkey is a small animal of eight to ten hands but larger varieties may be found, as, for instance, the elegant white Egyptian riding donkey and the huge animals used in the United States, France and Spain for mule-breeding, which can be up to fifteen or sixteen hands in height. The body colours are limited to a basic grey, white or brown. As to markings, dorsal and shoulder stripes are common but the irregular white markings, so frequently seen on the face and legs of the horse, are very rare indeed in the donkey.

In general social behaviour the ass is similar to the other members of the Equidae. It should perhaps be mentioned that the reputation of the jackass for sexual vigour is well deserved and that there was wisdom in the old army instruction: when in camp male and female donkeys should always be kept separate owing to the trouble liable to be created by their highly developed sexual instincts. But apart from that understandable trait, the donkey is a gentle friendly creature whose apparent stubbornness derives not so much from stupidity as from an intelligent determination to get its own way. According to travellers on the South African veld [52] the presence of donkeys in a camp has an irresistible attraction for zebras, which collect round the donkey kraals and create so much noise and excitement that the semi-terrified donkeys are liable to break loose and career over the country, whereupon they are chased, kicked and bitten by the zebras.

Chapter 8

Zebras

THE vivid striping of the zebras is in sharp distinction to the plainer coat of the horses and the asses but too much should not be made of this obvious difference because, even among members of a family, colour patterns may vary; for instance some types of zebra are less striped than others and some horses and asses may display quite marked striping. Hence Charles Darwin [15] and other writers after him thought it possible that all the existing races of *Equus* were descended from striped ancestors, which might lead to the assumption that the earlier types of horse looked very like the modern zebra. On the other hand Hopwood [30], as mentioned in chapter 4, postulated that zebras could not be immediately ancestral to the horse because the fossil record shows that the zebras were in the vanguard of the migration that brought *Equus* into the Old World and zebras were to be found in Europe before the horses made their appearance there; from this he deduced that the horses and the zebras evolved separately, probably while still in their North American homeland, from the species grouped together under the genera of *Pliohippus* and *Plesippus*. Certainly horses, asses and zebras have a very similar anatomical make-up and if it was not for some minor differences in their teeth it would be difficult from their fossil remains alone to distinguish between these species.

The European zebras died out during the Ice Age and now the group is found only in Africa where it is represented by three species: in northern Kenya and the scrub-covered deserts of Somaliland by the large ass-like Grevy's zebra, *Equus grevyi*: on the savannahs of eastern Africa and South Africa by the common zebra, *Equus burchelli*, a name that incorporates several local varieties differing somewhat in the pattern and the colouration of their coat, such as Grant's zebra, Boehm's zebra and Chapman's zebra; and in the mountains of the Cape and the coastal areas of South West Africa respectively, by the mountain zebras, *Equus zebra zebra* and *Equus zebra hartmannae.* Also, until about one hundred years ago, a fourth species existed in South Africa, the quagga, *Equus quagga.*

The quagga, a heavily built animal of thirteen to fourteen hands, was once plentiful in the south-eastern corner of the Cape. Its brown and white stripes were confined mostly to the head, neck and fore part of the body and in appearance it was rather a horse-like creature; and so docile and easy to domesticate that in the early nineteenth century an imported pair were driven regularly about London harnessed to a phaeton; and such was its courage that Boer farmers kept small herds of quaggas on their premises to protect the domestic livestock from marauding packs of wild dogs and hyaenas. In the wild, on the open plains where it usually grazed in company with the white-tailed gnu and with ostriches, the great herds of quagga were an impressive sight. Lydekker [49] quotes an attractive description of a typical scene on the veld: 'Moving slowly across the profile of the ocean-like horizon, uttering a shrill barking neigh, of which its name forms a correct imitation, long files of quagga continually remind the early traveller of a rival caravan on the march.'

However the slow-moving unwary quagga was an easy quarry for the Boer settlers who needed its meat to feed their native servants and by the middle of the nineteenth century it had been practically shot out of existence in the country to the south of the Orange River. Further north, in the Orange Free State, quaggas continued to flourish for a while until a profitable market developed for their hides, which were used for making grain sacks and articles of harness, and the species was finally exterminated by 1878, though, as Harper [26] mentions, it is difficult to obtain any accurate information on the subject as very often the quagga was confused with Burchell's zebra; in fact at that time the quagga was thought to be merely the southern form of Burchell's zebra, which being more fully striped than the quagga carried the name of bontequagga, meaning striped or painted quagga.

The typical Burchell's zebra, *Equus burchelli burchelli,* which had a striped head, neck and body but white unbanded limbs, died out by 1909, but the burchelline group of zebras remains very abundant on the savannahs of the south and east of Africa. These animals are fully striped on all parts of the body including the limbs, though naturally there are local variations in coat patterns. In northern Kenya there is the black and white striped Grant's zebra, *Equus burchelli granti*; in southern Kenya and Tanzania, Boehm's zebra, *Equus burchelli boehmi,* with brown shadow stripes in between the black and the white; and south of the Zambesi River, Chapman's zebra, *Equus burchelli chapmani*, which has particularly well marked shadow stripes. These zebras can be noisy animals and their barking cry 'qua-ha' has been described as not unlike that of a dog when heard at a distance. Klingel [32] has described six different vocal sounds: a contact call, two warning sounds, two expressions of pain and one of well-being.

In parts of northern Kenya the small Grant's zebra shares the grazing areas with the big Grevy's zebra; it is an amicable association and the two species show no inclination to compete for territory, fight for mares or to interbreed. Grevy's differs from most of the other zebras not only in its greater size and in its narrower stripes; but with its larger ears it is an altogether more ass-like desert-dwelling creature, albeit a very impressive one: so much so that the kings and emperors of Abyssinia were accustomed to sending specimens as ceremonial gifts to potentates in Europe and elsewhere. In fact Grevy's zebra owes its name to the French president who was honoured in this way in 1882. At the beginning of the Christian era it seems that this species of zebra was transported to Rome for exhibition as a curiosity in the amphitheatre, where it received the name of *Hippotigris*, a title that led to the myth that this strange striped creature was a cross between a horse and a tiger. Its voice is described by Lydekker [40] as a very hoarse kind of grunt, followed by a shrill whistling sound.

In their southern range the burchelline zebras overlap the territory of the mountain zebras but again with no tendency to intermix the species. The mountain zebras, or true zebras as they are sometimes called, show a distinctive transverse gridiron pattern of striping on their hind-quarters and carry a small dewlap on the throat; incidentally these characteristics are well shown on the painting made by George Stubbs in 1763 of a zebra which was the property of the then Prince of Wales, or perhaps his wife Princess Charlotte. In the early days of Cape Colony there seems to have been quite a trade with Mauritius in mountain zebras, which had been captured as foals and trained to harness; but generally the mountain zebras are considered to be less amenable to domestication than either of the other two species. It is normally a very shy and silent animal; when the voice is used it is a soft neigh or whinny, quite distinct from the raucous calls of the other zebras. In the Cape, the small active *Equus zebra zebra* has been saved from extinction by the establishment of the Mountain Zebra National Park but the larger sub-species *Equus zebra hartmannae* of South West Africa, although still plentiful, is rapidly declining in numbers despite being protected from unlicensed hunting. The main reasons are the increasing erection of long stretches of game-proof fencing, which sometimes cuts off the herds from their water supplies, and other measures taken to protect farm crops and grazing from the severe damage that zebras can cause at times.

The zebra is a fairly big powerful animal and it might be thought that the lion would be the only serious predator. But Van Lawick-Goodall [63] and others have shown that wild dogs and hyenas have to be reckoned with also, as packs of these animals will deliberately pursue zebras and tear to pieces any one of the herd that falls behind in the hunt, whether it be a foal or a sick or aged adult. It is possible that zebras derive some security from their habit of consorting with gnu, hartebeeste and ostrich, which give them early warning of danger; as well as from their own precautionary measures that include only resting-up in areas of short grass, where it is difficult to surprise them, with always at least one zebra on its feet acting as a sentry and ready to give the alarm at any suspicious approach. The main defence however lies in the organization of a closely knit family unit.

Klingel [32] in his prolonged study of the habits of the burchelline zebras noted that even the largest herds, which can number over a hundred thousand, were made up of small coherent family groups of not more than sixteen animals, together with a few all-male groups of similar size. The occasional solitary animals that were seen were invariably male. The typical family group consists of a stallion with four or five mares and their young; the stallion is dominant but when on the move it is a mare that leads and the stallion brings up the rear. When threatened by predators the groups join up in the course of their flight and the pursuers have to try to penetrate a bunched-up herd, guarded behind and on its flanks by very aggressive stallions.

The family group is fairly stable; the mares remain with it all their lives, and only an old or sick stallion is likely to be replaced by another male. The fillies mature at around two years of age and then leave either to form the nucleus of a new family or to enter an existing one. At about the same period in life the young males wander off to form bachelor groups until such a time as they can find their own mares and start their own families.

The stallions fight viciously over young mares in oestrus but serious permanent injury is seldom inflicted by the stylized methods of combat that include neck-wrestling, kicking and biting. And within families there seems to be a strong social bond: sick and weak animals are not chased away but are likely to be helped and protected. Van Lawick-Goodall [63] describes one instance in which a troop of zebras returned to rescue a mare and foal that had been cut out of the herd by hyenas.

Chapter 9

Hybrids

THERE are many accounts of domestic mares being driven off by wild horse stallions to become members of wild herds where they have bred normally; also, man has sometimes deliberately used the wild horse to reinvigorate his domestic stock, just as African tribesmen have been known to leave their donkey mares out in the desert in order to attract the services of the wild ass. Such crosses of wild horse with domestic horse and wild ass with donkey produces healthy fertile offspring, a fact that has been proved often in zoos under controlled conditions, and there is no instinctive social bar to these matings between different varieties of the same species.

However in the wild a natural antipathy exists to matings between the different species of the genus *Equus*. Thus though their territories may overlap, the three species of zebra show no inclination to interbreed; likewise in their shared grazing areas, Grevy's zebra and the wild ass keep to their own kind; and there are no authentic records of interbreeding between the Przewalski horse and hemionus on their native steppes and deserts.

The aversion to mating with another species can be largely overcome by various methods of habituation and training. For instance it is customary to rear a jack-donkey intended for mule-breeding in company with young horses and never to allow him to consort with other donkeys or to serve a donkey mare. Other customs include the bizarre *lalandage*, once employed in the mule-breeding districts of Poitou: a sort of encouraging erotic chorus chanted by the studsmen as they stand around the reluctant jack and his intended mate. The stallion mates even less readily with the she-ass and the conception rate of this cross is said to be low, possibly because the horse has a shorter penis than the jack. The male zebra and the male hemionus are stated to mate quite readily with the other equine species, though some individuals may be difficult. The extensive literature on mammalian hybrids has been summarized by Gray [24] whose survey shows that reciprocal crosses between all the equine species are possible but that the resultant offspring are almost invariably sterile.

By far the commonest equine hybrids are the mule (jack-ass × mare) and the hinny or jennet (horse × she-ass), which have been bred extensively over many centuries for both military and civilian employment. Their size depends largely on the size of their dams, so the mule is generally bigger than the hinny; otherwise the two hybrids are very similar in appearance, having a varied mixture of horse-like and donkey-like characteristics. In temperament they mostly resemble the donkey with their self-willed nature that responds affectionately to sympathetic treatment and sometimes with explosive violence to ignorant handling. The economic handicap of their lack of breeding ability is more than balanced by the advantages of their toughness and endurance and by their resistance to disease, which is greater than that of either parent.

This hybrid vigour is the main reason for the remarkable popularity of the mule as a work animal, a fact that is well brought out in the official statistics of the British Army Veterinary Services for World War I [8] which state:

The mule proved far more resistant than the horse to adverse circumstances of animal management, just as he proved superior in every veterinary respect: mortality among mules consequent upon transportation by land and sea was less than half that among horses; mortality from disease and all causes in the field was less than half that among horses; liability to disease (including mange) necessitating evacuation to veterinary hospitals was less than half that among horses; the mule could be kept in good condition on a food ration that was 25 per cent less than the average of the horse.

Cross-breeding between hemionus and the horse and hemionus and the ass produces hybrids said to be superior to mules in some respects but temperamentally less suited to domestication: there was always an element of wildness in their nature that could probably only be eliminated by a long programme of selective breeding. In chapter 5 mention was made of an experiment, designed to refute the suggestion that the Przewalski horse was merely a chance hybrid between hemionus and a feral Mongolian pony, in which an Indian ghor-khar, *Equus hemionus khur*, was mated with three types of pony mare: a Mongolian, an Exmoor and a Shetland-Welsh. The resultant hybrids were exceptionally active vigorous animals, but quite unlike the Przewalski both in their appearance and in their sterility.

The same geneticist, Cossar Ewart [18], undertook another somewhat

44

similar project, this time to test the validity of the ancient theory of telegony that assumes that the male parent puts his stamp not only on his own progeny but also on all subsequent offspring out of that female by any sire. For instance it was, and sometimes still is, thought that once a pedigree bitch has mated with a mongrel dog she is useless for pedigree breeding ever after; conversely it was considered wise to start a young mare's stud life by putting her to an exceptionally good stallion in the hope that his influence would benefit all her progeny throughout her breeding career. The classic example of telegony, reported to the Royal Society by Lord Morton and believed even by Darwin at one stage, involved an Arab mare that had been mated to a quagga and then in subsequent pregnancies by an Arab stallion continued to produce foals with striped markings. The fact that a degree of striping is not uncommon in the horse was overlooked. Ewart attempted to reproduce the phenomenon, using a Burchell's zebra in place of a quagga, and came merely to the conclusion that if there was such a thing as telegony at all then it must be of rare occurrence.

Of course now the theory has been discarded as a mere superstition, but at the time the publicity given to the experiment focused attention on the possibilities of using zebra hybrids in the tsetse-fly belts and horse-sickness areas of Africa where horses could not survive for long, and of drawing on the vast herds of wild zebras as a source of supply of transport animals for the tropical countries generally. For a while schemes for the domestication and hybridization of zebras were pursued actively in several countries, including Russia, France and South Africa, but with only qualified success. The zebra hybrids resulting from matings with either the horse or the ass all showed a variable amount of striping; some of the hybrids were good workers and easily managed, others were described as bad tempered, easily panicked and apt to kick out at everything in sight.

It is such a rarity for a mule, or any equine hybrid, to produce a foal that the event was once regarded as unnatural and of ill-omen. Many of the old reports of such happenings may, as Tegetmeier and Sutherland [58] have suggested, relate either to mules that have adopted stray orphan foals or to pregnancies in horses or asses that happen to have a vaguely mulish appearance. However the possibility of a fertile hybrid cannot be ruled out completely. Gray [24], in a summary of recent literature on the subject, states that usually the mule and the hinny are sterile in both sexes but the females may come on heat and occasionally may produce foals to either the stallion or the jack-ass. On the other hand there are no records of fertile male mules or hinnies. Generally the semen of the male hybrid is a milky

45

liquid containing at the most a few non-motile spermatozoa though the sexual drive appears to be normal. Both the well-marked libido and the inhibition of sperm production may be due to the excess of androgen-producing Leydig cells found in the mule testes. In general it seems to be true that all the equine hybrids of both sexes give every indication of sexual activity, but no offspring are produced from matings between the hybrids, or as a rule between hybrids and the parental species.

The crossing of two species gives the offspring an uneven number of chromosomes and it is probably this imbalance that usually leads to an imperfect development of the reproductive system and consequent sterility. Thus the domestic horse with 64 chromosomes when crossed with the ass with 62 chromosomes gives a mule or hinny with 63 chromosomes; or when crossed with Grevy's zebra with 46 chromosomes, produces a hybrid with 55 chromosomes; and the ass when mated to a common zebra with 44 chromosomes gives a hybrid with 53 chromosomes. However the Przewalski horse with 66 chromosomes when mated to the domestic horse gives perfectly fertile offspring with 65 chromosomes so clearly an odd number of chromosomes does not always cause sterility.

Chapter 10

The Origins of the Domestic Horse

WHEN the Ice Age ended the periglacial tundra and grasslands of Western Europe, where thousands of wild horses once grazed, were replaced by dense forests, an unsatisfactory environment for horses, which therefore withdrew to the more congenial plains and steppes of Eastern Europe and Asia. Other smaller groups of wild horses survived in the northern and central parts of the European continent. India was without wild horses at this period, Britain also; and they were missing from the fauna of the eastern Mediterranean, the Middle East and Africa.

It is true that some evidence, based chiefly on rock pictures of uncertain age, has been put forward for the survival in postglacial Spain and north-western Africa, of a robust forest-adapted horse believed by some to have been the ancestor of the large 'cold-blooded' horses of Europe. Rather better evidence suggests, however, that this race, *Equus germanicus*, became extinct in western Europe during the Ice Age; Zeuner [67], after a careful assessment of all the facts, came to the conclusion that 'more than anywhere else this race has bred in the minds of those who thought that the large and heavy cold-blooded horses of the west and north Europe required an ancestor different from that of the slender Arab. That breeding for size is possible in other domesticated animals is well known and it is unwise to introduce size into the hypothetical phylogeny of the domestic horse.'

However the postglacial survivors in northern Europe may, it seems, have been of a heavier type than wild horses elsewhere, not that this means that they represent a separate species: local geographical variations in form are almost inevitable in animals with as wide a range as the horse. In fact it is fairly certain that the only true horses to survive into the postglacial period were of the species *Equus caballus przewalskii*, a species that is generally acknowledged to be ancestral to the tarpan and to all the domestic breeds in all their variety.

Cole [12] states that animal domestication was known in northern Iraq by 8900 BC, sheep being the first species to be kept in this manner. The new agricultural system gradually took in cattle, goats and pigs, and its practice spread to other parts with the migration of neolithic peoples from the Middle East in two main directions: up the Danube and across central Europe, reaching Germany and the Netherlands by 4500 BC; and along the shores and islands of the Mediterranean to Spain and the Atlantic coast, reaching Britain by 3200 BC. At much the same period a similar agricultural economy based on grain crops and domesticated animals developed in China. It is probable that this primitive form of farming was an essential prelude to the domestication of the horse: a technique that began around 3000 BC in the region of Turkestan and on the steppes of southern Russia and was carried round the known world in the Bronze Age, during the second millennium BC, mostly through the processes of war and the migration of people and also, to some extent, by trade.

In 3000 BC there were few if any horses, either wild or tame, in the Middle East and the ancient Egyptians had only oxen and donkeys to use as work animals, to haul their carts and, occasionally, to ride. But in Mesopotamia the Sumerians had learned to exploit the speed of the onager for warlike purposes: they employed two sorts of war-chariot, both of which were drawn by four onagers, yoked four abreast and controlled like oxen by nose-rings. There was the two-wheeled scouting-chariot for one man, who sat uncomfortably astride the centre pole on a sort of saddle; and a four-wheeled battle-chariot, carrying a driver equipped with a goad and a soldier armed with an axe and javelins. These chariots had solid wheels fixed to the axle and, teamed as they were by unruly onagers, must have been very hard to manoeuvre. Indeed Noble [44] suggests that the battle-chariot must have been used as a sort of guided missile:

We may consider that the onagers were pointed in the desired direction and held by the grooms until the opportune moment when they were launched against the foe. The soldier's axe and spear can only have been used for personal defence as the four animals would cut a swathe two and a half metres wide through the enemy and any persons within reach would have been trampled over. As the enemy line was approached the spearman can have had time to throw only two spears before the chariot passed through the opposing forces or was brought to a standstill. The real weapon was the onagers' hooves and the effect was psychological rather than material.

Despite their clumsiness these early chariots were valuable weapons. The later chariots of the second millennium BC proved even more effective: so much so that they dominated the battlefields for hundreds of years and history abounds with descriptions of the triumphs of the chariots of the Assyrians, the Hittites, the Egyptians, the Greeks, the Persians and others. Their success owed much to the combination of two innovations: the substitution of a spoked wheel rotating on the axle for the old block wheel, and the replacement of the almost unsteerable onager by the more amenable horse. In skilled hands the horse chariot could be used for a variety of purposes in open country: for a direct charge to break the opposing line, for the swift pursuit of a fleeing enemy, and for the rapid deployment of forces both before and during a battle. A large well-trained contingent of chariotry was considered an essential part of most Bronze Age armies and good horses were much prized and in great demand.

But the first appearance of the horse on the Middle Eastern scene was in a fairly peaceful and unspectacular role: pulling the little wagons of the gypsy-like Aryan migrants who, at the end of the third millennium BC, had trekked down from the north of the Caspian, through the mountains of the Caucasus and Armenia, to infiltrate most of the eastern Mediterranean area. These people brought with them not only the horses that became the nucleus of the breeding stock of this previously horseless region but also, most likely because they must have been expert wheelwrights, the idea for the design of the new spoke-wheeled chariot. A similar Aryan migration in about 1500 BC took the horse to India.

Drower [16] states that the first mention of the horse in literature occurs in a text of the Third Dynasty of Ur, *circa* 2100 BC, in which the animal is described as 'the ass of the mountains or foreign ass, of the caravan route, with flowing tail'. Oddly enough the Hammurabi Code, written about three hundred years later, has nothing to say concerning horses though it goes into great detail on such matters as the exact fee payable to a veterinary surgeon who treats an ox or an ass successfully and the exact fine he must pay if his treatment results in the death of his patient. If the Babylonians were really so ignorant of the use of the horse then it is easy to understand how it was, in 1594 BC, that a chariot force of the Hittites was able to surprise their army and to leave Babylon in ruins.

The Hittites of Anatolia and their neighbours, the Mitanni, were of Aryan origin and skilled in horse breeding and chariot fighting, perhaps the originators of the large-scale military use of this new technique which of dire necessity was quickly adopted by the other peoples in that part of the world. The resulting very considerable military requirements for horses could be met only partially by trade within the Middle East and by imports from the Caucasus and the north, and for this reason horse breeding became of importance where suitable grazing areas could be found for the brood mares and their young. At a rather later period in history, for instance, Herodotus [29] says that the Satrap of Assyria had sixteen thousand mares at stud with eight hundred stallions. Much the same pattern of development occurred in India, though it relied more heavily than the Middle East on large droves of young horses being brought in regularly each year from central Asia. The value of the chariot horse and the care and attention lavished on it may be gauged from such treatises as that of Kikkuli of Mitanni who, in the fourteenth century BC, gave authoritative instruction on the lengthy programme of conditioning and graduated exercise that should be followed with remounts to make them ready for army service.

The use of the chariot horse spread to the whole of the Mediterranean area, including Greece, Crete and Italy, and among other places the plains of Thessaly became an important breeding centre, its horses being noted for their courage and endurance, as shown by such renowned animals as the Thessalian-bred chariot horses of Achilles and Orestes, and by Alexander's charger, Bucephalus, which carried the great king in many of his victories and finally died of battle wounds at the age of thirty.

To the south, Egypt and Libya were well known for their chariot horses and Cyrene was an excellent horse-breeding area. From Cyrenaica, charioteers spread westwards along the coast and also far inland, across the Sahara to Mali. Lhote [36], from a study of a large series of Saharan rock-drawings, has traced the route of the chariots from Tripoli through Ghadames and the Tassili and Hoggar highlands to Gao on the river Niger. The earlier paintings show the usual two-wheeled chariots drawn by pairs of horses, some later pictures are of huge four-horse chariots and then at around 600 BC the chariots are replaced by ridden horses, which in their turn give way to camels. Lhote associates these chariot people with the ancient Garamentes, whom Herodotus described as hunting the Ethiopian hole-men or troglodytes in four-horse chariots 'for these troglodytes are exceedingly swift of foot', and thinks that the modern Touaregs are their descendants.

For much of the second millennium BC the chariot horse remained the small active type of pony originally introduced from the north by the Aryan invaders. It was perfectly possible to ride these little animals but their use for military purposes was limited by the fact that they could not carry the weight of an armed soldier for very long; and apart from this, riding was considered undignified: well enough for stableboys and the like but quite unsuited to warriors and men of importance. Nevertheless chariotry could not operate in rough or mountainous country, which mounted troops could traverse with ease, and when, at about 1400 BC, bigger horses became available cavalry units soon came into being, rendering the chariot obsolescent on the battlefield, though for hundreds of years it continued in use for many sacred, ceremonial and sporting occasions; and in isolated areas, for war also, as Julius Caesar discovered when he invaded Britain and had to admit in his despatches that even for his experienced men fighting against chariots could be very dangerous work indeed.

At first under domestication animals tend to degenerate and become smaller than their wild ancestors but the horse was an exception to this rule, probably because it was better fed and cared for than other livestock. And no doubt among the well-tended grain-fed chariot horses some exceptional animals appeared that were used to improve the size and performance of the race in general. Incidentally barley was the usual grain for feeding to horses. Other rideable horses were introduced to the Middle East about 900 BC by a second Aryan invasion of mounted nomads who settled in the regions of Iran, Media and Parthia. All these areas became notable for the horses they produced, particularly the Nisaean breed, which had the uncomfortable reputation of being of great size and with feet that shake the earth. Thus as the physique of horses improved during the first millennium BC, so riding became fairly general in those parts of Europe, Asia and North Africa where previously the horse-drawn vehicle had predominated. The new development was of great historic importance for a number of reasons, not least among them being the great mobility it gave to the nomad hordes inhabiting the vast grasslands that lie between Western Europe and China, enabling them to raid virtually where they pleased in a manner reminiscent of the Vikings, sweeping in from the sea on any unguarded coast.

Herodotus [29] gives a good idea of how difficult it was to defeat the nomads in his description of the Scythians, one of the most famous of the steppe-peoples: 'A people without fortified towns, living in wagons which they take with them wherever they go, accustomed, one and all, to fight on horseback with bows and arrows, and dependent for their food not upon agriculture but upon their cattle: how can such people fail to defeat the attempt of an invader not only to subdue them but even to make contact with them.' In fact a raiding force of nomads was even more mobile and elusive than Herodotus suggests: each nomad had about a dozen horses that could graze and forage for themselves while the man at a pinch could live on their blood and the milk of the mares and be independent of other food supplies. The dependence of the horses on grazing was however sometimes a handicap: after a long hard winter they would be suffering from semi-starvation and this was the traditional time for the settled communities to strike at the nomads – when their horses were too weak to move far or fast.

It is not known for certain how the Chinese acquired their knowledge of horse breeding and chariotry but there is a strong probability that it came to them from the steppe-people, kinsmen of the nomads who introduced the horse to the Middle East and India. Unlike those countries, however, China possessed its own indigenous herds of wild horses and it was from these Przewalski-type animals that the Chinese bred their chariot horses. From the first appearance of the domestic horse in China, *circa* 1500 BC, the animal had some mystic significance: chariot horses are found buried with emperors in the royal tombs and there was even a special cemetery containing the remains of chariot horses. Zeuner [67] thinks that the burials accorded to horses indicate that they were regarded as comrades rather than slaves, a feeling shared by the horsemen of many other nations and one that may account for the rather general widespread taboo on eating the flesh of the domestic horse.

The main employment of the Chinese chariotry was to counter the ceaseless raids of the nomads on the northern borders: this entailed a lot of hard fighting and in their efforts to get the upper hand and remove this threat to their existence, the Chinese throughout the first millennium BC made many improvements in their weaponry and military tactics. Of particular interest was the invention of a new type of harness; Tregear [60] states that excavations of Chou burials of the fourth century BC show the usual spoke-wheel chariots and Przewalski-type horses but instead of the old choker style harness that pressed on the windpipe and jugular veins there is a breast-strap harness that allows the horse to take the strain more effectively on the shoulders and chest. This antedates the appearance of such harness in Europe by some seven centuries and would account for the very effective Chinese chariot fighting of the period. But the nomads had by now learnt to use mounted men and their incursions had become even more dangerous, among other things threatening to cut off the Chinese from their main horse-producing areas. The Chinese horses were no better than those of the nomads and the shortage of fast light-cavalry horses with which to beat the nomads at their own game was a serious weakness.

1. Palaeolithic cave painting of a wild horse from the Dordogne, France. At this period, towards the end of the Ice Age, the wild horse was abundant in western Europe and extensively hunted for food. The species was probably ancestral to *Equus przewalskii*.

2. BELOW The Przewalski horse. The only true wild horse in existence. It is thought to be the ancestor of all modern breeds of horse. Until recently the species was relatively common in Mongolia and adjoining territories.

3. RIGHT Somali wild ass. The African wild asses are larger and more donkey-like than those of Asia. The leg stripes are typical of the Somali wild ass; the Nubian race and the domestic donkey usually show a well-marked shoulder stripe.

4. LEFT Onagers, the Persian variety of the Asiatic wild ass. It has close relatives in the kiang of Tibet, the kulan of Mongolia and the ghor-khur of Pakistan. The Syrian race of wild ass, the wild ass of the bible, is probably extinct.

5. LEFT Donkey and foal.

. LEFT Grevy's zebra. Its large size, long slender skull, large ears and vivid striping distinguish this species from the other zebras. Grevy's zebra possesses a number of very primitive anatomical characteristics that are similar to those found in the zebroid equids of the early Pleistocene, such as *Equus stenonis*.

. RIGHT Quagga. Once extremely common throughout southern Africa, this species of zebra has now been extinct for about one hundred years. The specimen in this picture died at the London zoo in 1872.

. RIGHT Mountain zebra. There are two varieties; a small stocky animal originating from the highlands of Cape colony and the larger Hartmann's mountain zebra found in mountain ranges of the sea-board of south-west Africa. Both varieties include among their distinguishing features a typical grid-iron pattern of stripes on the rump and a small dew-lap in the centre of the neck.

9. LEFT Burchell's zebra. This is a prolific group of zebras, common throughout east and south-east Africa. Also known as the plains zebra or bonte-quagga. Owing to the great variety of striping and colour within the group, as many as twenty sub-species have been named.

10. RIGHT A hybrid foal, the offspring of a quagga stallion and a mare. All the equine species can interbreed but the offspring are almost invariably sterile.

11. ABOVE Welsh mountain ponies. One of the most popular of the many native British breeds of pony. Arab and other foreign blood has been introduced into nearly all the pony breeds from time to time but essentially they differ little from their ancestors which have bred on the moorlands and hills of Britain for hundreds of years.

12. BELOW Shetland pony. The smallest and probably the purest and most ancient of the pony breeds of Britain.

13. OPPOSITE Horses of the King's Troop, Royal Horse Artillery. These are mostly half-bred horses of the hunter stamp bred in Ireland.

14. OPPOSITE ABOVE Nasrullah. A good example of the thoroughbred. A stallion of exceptional merit; during the 1950's he was champion sire both in the USA and in Britain.

15. The Byerley Turk. The first of the three foundation stallions from which all thoroughbreds are descended. It is thought that he may have been of Turkmene blood.

16. The Darley Arabian. The second foundation stallion. He is known without question to have been a pure-bred Arab.

17. OPPOSITE BELOW The Arab. The breed is made up of a number of strains or families, all of them of eastern origin but now spread world-wide. Among other things they have been used extensively to improve native breeds and to help in the formation of new breeds.

18. The Godolphin Arabian. The third foundation stallion. His breeding is uncertain but reputedly he came from Barbary and there are good grounds for thinking that he was a Barb.

19. OPPOSITE Suffolk Punch. One of the oldest of the British draught breeds; it was developed for farm work on heavy soils as well as for road haulage.

20. RIGHT AND BELOW Orlov trotter. A fast strong general purpose harness horse developed in Russia during the eighteenth century from an Arab-Dutch cross.

21. OPPOSITE Clydesdale. A powerful heavy draught horse developed in Scotland during the eighteenth century from a smaller breed of pack-horse.

22. RIGHT Percheron. Originally a fast active harness horse with Arab blood. It has since been developed into a heavy draught horse which is very popular both in its homeland, France, and in the Americas.

23. Don mare and foal. This breed provided the traditional mounts of the Don cossacks. During the nineteenth century Arab and thoroughbred blood was introduced to give bigger and speedier horses. Dons are still reared in herds on the steppes bordering the Black Sea.

24. BELOW Kazakh. The hardy steppe pony of Kazakhistan.

25. BELOW RIGHT Mongolian pony. This type of animal has a wide distribution over the Asiatic steppes and highlands. One of the most primitive forms of domestic horse.

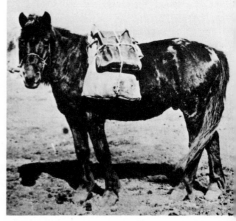

26. ABOVE Akhal-teke. One of the ancient breeds of Turkmenistan. Valued for its speed and powers of endurance. The Byerley Turk may have been of this blood.

27. LEFT Yakut. A horse well adapted to the bitter cold of the Russian arctic. It is used for all purposes, from meat and milk production to riding and harness work.

28. RIGHT Mustangs. A group of feral horses in the foothills of Montana, USA.

29. BELOW Pinto. The coloured pony, skewbald or piebald, of the American West. Held in high regard by Red Indian and cowhand alike.

30. TOP Appaloosa. A spotted breed developed from Spanish horses by the Nez Percé Indians and now bred extensively in America and Europe.

31. ABOVE Palamino. The name denotes a colour rather than a breed. The colour, a golden coat with silver mane and tail, does not breed true.

32. LEFT Morgan. An excellent breed of general purpose horse of mixed English and Spanish ancestry tracing back in the paternal line to the stallion Justin Morgan which died in Vermont, USA, in 1821.

33. ABOVE Quarter
horse. Developed in the
eastern states of the
USA during the
eighteenth century from
an Anglo-Spanish cross,
this clever powerful
little horse spread
westward and was
considered ideal for
work on the cattle
ranches. It now enjoys
a world-wide popularity
as a riding horse.

34. LEFT Tennessee
walking horse. A breed
deliberately designed to
provide a safe and very
comfortable ride.
Numerous breeds went
into its make-up,
including thoroughbred
Arab and Morgan.

No doubt with the purpose of easing their remount problem, the Chinese in 102 BC sent a military expedition to Ferghana, a city state in Turkestan, to obtain a supply of the 'superior' horses of that region, which from all accounts were the same type of light fast animals as those taken by the Aryans to the Middle East nearly two thousand years before. The expedition returned not only with three thousand superior horses but also with thirty 'heavenly' horses. The latter had certain mystic attributes: they sweated blood when under a hot sun, in this world they could cover three hundred miles a day at a gallop and in the next they could carry a human soul to the Holy Mountain and the Land of Perpetual Peace.

An important innovation that radically altered cavalry tactics was the use of stirrups, giving the rider a firmer seat and a better control of his mount and enabling him to wield a long heavy lance. This came to China between the second and fourth centuries AD and was probably copied from the nomad Sarmatians. Phillips [47], describing the military equipment of these people at about the fourth century BC, says:

The use of leather foot thongs begins among these cavalry, who needed them to give a firmer seat to the mounted lancer, and so also does a new form of attack in close ranks of riders equivalent to a mounted phalanx. With such equipment and tactics the Sarmatians next drove the Royal Hordes of the Scythians of the Pontic Steppes into their later refuges in the Crimea and the Dobrudja. This manner of fighting was also adopted by the nomads of the Gobi and by the Chinese. It became characteristic of the whole Iranian world, both settled and nomadic for some centuries.

Bigger heavy cavalry horses were now needed and the Chinese obtained them chiefly from the Iranian state of Parthia. In fact during the early part of the Christian era there were regular imports of horses from a variety of places. Neve [43] writes of the eighth century AD:

Enormous numbers of diplomatic missions from all Asia and the Middle East came to the imperial court with presents and curiosities, and more often than not with horses. The most prized were from the breeding centres of Khotan and Ferghana, and in the time of Min Huang in the 720s and '30s there are reported to have been 40,000 horses in the imperial stables. The emperor selected the best of them and treated them like his Chinese coursers. Of all of them he had portraits made, describing how the horses were sent in relays from foreign lands, crossing wide stretches of desert that wore their hooves thin. The most popular types had romantic names, Fire Blossom, Drifting Cloud, Flying Yellow, Night Lightening.

To the far west of the steppes there were no early civilizations comparable to those of China and the Middle East, simply rather unsophisticated farming communities and pastoral tribes dependent for their livelihood on cereals, domestic cattle, sheep and pigs, and on hunting. These people received their first knowledge of the domestic horse and of wheeled vehicles from the battle-axe people, so called from their custom of burying stone battle-axes with the warrior dead, who had migrated from the southern Russian steppes to reach central and northern Europe during the second millennium BC. In Europe, as in China, the indigenous wild horse herds provided the foundation domestic breeding stock and it would have been these European-bred animals that, some hundreds of years later, reached western Europe and Britain. Ferrying horses across the sea in the light craft then available cannot have been easy and for a long time horses remained something of a rarity here in Britain and therefore perhaps used more for peaceful haulage rather than for hazardous war-like ploys.

However during the second century BC the Belgae, a people of mixed Celtic and German descent, crossed the Channel, bringing with them chariots and horses. It was these war-like tribes that opposed Julius Caesar with chariots and cavalry when he invaded Britain in 55 and 54 BC. Their horses are likely to have been of mixed European, steppe and Mediterranean blood as, on the Continent, the Celts traded with Greeks, Italians and Scythians and willingly paid high prices for any good horses that they found. Unlike the Germans, who according to Caesar [9] staunchly resisted all foreign influences:

They are content with their home-bred horses, which, although undersized and ugly, are rendered capable of very hard work by daily exercise. In cavalry battles they often dismount and fight on foot, training the horses to stand perfectly still, so that they can quickly get back to them in case of need. In their eyes it is the height of effeminacy and shame to use a saddle and they do not hesitate to engage the largest force of cavalry riding saddled horses, however small their own numbers may be.

Later on during the Roman occupation of Britain, horses were imported from all parts of the empire to mount the cavalry that were mostly recruited from Gaul and Germany but included Sarmatian, Spanish and Swiss units.

A similar mingling of horses from many different countries occurred throughout the Roman dominions and over the centuries a mixing process was maintained by the ebb and flow of military adventures across the known world. Among them were the invasion of Gaul and Italy in the fifth century AD by the mounted hordes of Attila the Hun, and the many successes of the horsemen of holy Islam that were halted only in Europe when the Arabs at last met defeat at the hands of the Frankish armies on the field of Poitiers in AD 732. At this time the stallion was the preferred mount for a cavalryman and the almost continual transcontinental movement of tens of thousands of mature fully sexed animals of different origins, shapes and sizes must have made it impossible to establish fixed breeds in any save the most isolated regions. Nevertheless a number of national varieties of horse were developing at this period and from a study of the works of ancient authors Anderson [2] has drawn the following conclusions:

On the eve of the Moslem invasions the Arabs had developed a magnificent breed of light horses, the ancestors of the modern Arab, and far superior to anything else anywhere. This breed had developed within Arabia during the preceding seven or eight centuries, before which the horse was unknown there.

At the same time the light breeds of classical Europe had degenerated into worthless, flashy creatures. In the harder conditions of North Africa, a tougher race had survived. The barbarian invasions, which had over-run most of the western provinces of the empire had introduced a lot of Central Asiatic blood, though heavy cavalry, the ancestors of the mediaeval knights and contemporaries of Arthur's Round Table, certainly continued to flourish.

In the eastern provinces and in the Persian empire good heavy cavalry horses were still bred. But their armoured riders lacked the mobility of the Arab light cavalry, and, once battle was joined, were unable to close with them and to crush them.

On the whole, at this period in history, the horses of Europe were an indifferent lot, horse breeding was a neglected art and good stallions were more likely to be used as chargers than put to stud. But in Spain it was a different story: here during the Moorish occupation, which extended into the time of Columbus, a fast sturdy type of cavalry horse was bred in the province of Andalusia that owed many of its good qualities to a strong infusion of the tough North African strain. It was in the form of this Andalusian breed that the horse returned to the American continent from which it had disappeared so suddenly and strangely ten thousand years before.

After the discovery of the New World in 1492, a horsebreeding and acclimatization centre was established in the West Indies, which was the base for the early Spanish expeditions to South America, to Mexico and to Florida. The first horses to reach the mainland were the sixteen that Hernando Cortes took with him in 1519 as part of the little force that overthrew the Aztec empire and conquered Mexico. In the first two battles four horses were killed and the remainder severely wounded but Cortes owed much of his success to the terrified awe that these animals inspired in the Aztecs. In his *La Conquista de Nueva España*, Bernal Diaz, who accompanied the expedition, has lovingly described the colours and attributes of each of these precious animals: they were trusted comrades, known by name and by sight to all, it is unthinkable that they could ever have been lost or turned loose to run wild in this foreign land. Other horses were of course added to the expedition as reinforcements arrived from the West Indies and from Spain; less care may have been taken of these and at any rate under active-service conditions with numbers of horses it is inevitable that some will go astray: in this case perhaps to provide the first ancestors of the mustangs of Mexico and regions further north. Much the same pattern developed some years later in Pizarro's conquest of Peru when, like the Aztecs, the Incas were filled with consternation and panic at the sight of a few mounted men.

Ridgeway [48] asserts that the *baguales*, the feral horses that until recently swarmed in great herds of twenty thousand and more on the South American pampas, are all descended from the Andalusian horses introduced by the Spaniards in 1535 when the city of Buenos Ayres was founded. Following an Indian attack the settlement was abandoned in haste and five mares and seven stallions were left behind. When the Spaniards returned forty-five years later they found that a considerable herd had sprung up. A similar disaster to the town of San Juan Bautista in 1553 led to other horses being turned loose north of the river La Plata and, in the course of time despite all the hazards of life in the wild, led to the formation of other immense herds.

It is usually accepted that the first horses to colonize western America were those abandoned in 1542 by De Soto's ill-fated expedition to Florida. Apparently the Spaniards were fighting their way down the Mississippi, carrying twenty-two horses in their boats and making such slow progress that it was decided to jettison the horses on shore where, it is related, 'the Indians went unto them after the Spaniards were embarked – the horses were not acquainted with them and began to neigh and run up and down in such sort that the Indians, for fear of them, leaped into the water, and getting into their canoes went after the brigandines, shooting cruelly at them'.

The Indians soon lost their fear of horses and, as the herds of mustang grew in numbers and moved slowly northwards, tribe after tribe of the western plains adopted ways of living, fighting and hunting that depended almost entirely on the horse; and as mounted men they became almost as formidable a threat to the existence of the European settlers as the Scythians and other steppe-nomads had been in earlier times to the settled peoples of Eurasia.

Summerhays [57] describes the original mustang thus:

... a small horse, seldom more than 14.2 hands in height and from 600 to 800 lb. in weight. In common with all these small utility breeds, whether in the East or the West, they were nothing much to look at, scraggy and rough, of uncertain temper, but hardy and courageous, and apparently built of cast iron. Occasional throwbacks to their original remote Arabian ancestry were known to appear, becoming legendary figures for their outstanding size, beauty and speed. Every known colour was represented and many strange shades and combinations, of which again only the East has the like to show. Once broken and domesticated the mustang was a useful light saddle-horse, and was the original cow-pony.

Let us return to the other side of the world, where the requirements of Dutch and British colonists had created a demand for horses in South Africa, Australia and New Zealand.

The central African forests and tsetse-fly belts had inhibited any natural infiltration of horses from the north to the south that might otherwise have occurred and in Africa, as in other places, a good deal of the movement of horses depended on sea-borne traffic. In the seventeenth century The Dutch East India Company shipped into South Africa for the use of its settlers, horses of North African and Arab origin. Later shipments from England, Spain and the United States followed and the repeated inter-crossing of these various strains gave rise to the hardy Cape horse and the Basuto pony. However a number of factors, including the presence of many predatory animals and the mortality caused by the endemic insect-borne African horse sickness, limited the development of South Africa as a horse-breeding country.

Australasia, which had never numbered any of the Equidae among its fauna, received its first horses in 1795, in shipments from the Cape and from South America. Later arrivals included Arabs and English thorough-breds. Interbreeding of all these varieties gave rise to the typical Australian riding horse, the 'Waler', so-called because it originated in New South Wales. Despite periodical severe droughts, many parts of Australia are well suited to the horse and, with no endemic equine diseases to limit their multiplication, animals that escaped into the wild would often form large

57

feral herds, or in Australian parlance 'mobs of brumbies', which were a great nuisance to the stockmen. Ridgeway [48] quotes two examples: one, a herd of dwarfed cart-horses descended from the light-draught horses of the mid-nineteenth-century gold prospectors; and another, more elegant mob whose good looks could be traced to the services of an escaped Persian stallion. Another import, which proved very successful as a stock-pony in western Australia, was the Timor pony from Indonesia. It seems likely that Arab seamen operating from the Persian Gulf and Aden supplied not only India but also many of the Indonesian islands with horses from as early as the fourteenth century and, in considering the distribution of the domestic horse, due credit must be given to these ubiquitous traders in the East.

Chapter 11

Some Breeds of Europe and America

ALL modern horses are descended from the same tap-root of wild ancestors but, as with other species including man, different environments encouraged the development of different types of animal. The primary Asiatic centre of domestication produced the little wagon-horses that gave rise eventually to the graceful chariot horses depicted on the monuments of the ancient world; while the secondary northern European and Mongolian centres of domestication produced somewhat heavier animals approximating more closely to the original wild form of the Przewalski horse. These early varieties interbred indiscriminately as migrating and warring peoples spread over the world, taking their horses with them.

Deliberate cross-breeding was also practised in early times, usually with the objective of increasing the size and speed of the local animals. The Chinese and the Gauls, among others, were well aware of the value of importing new blood from places such as Ferghana, Parthia and Thessaly. But even those famous breeding areas produced local varieties rather than definite breeds of horse. Thus Parthian horses derived their name merely from their country of origin and not from any special lineage that identified them as a separate breed.

The advantage of segregating selected animals of proven ability into a closed group for breeding purposes is that with ensuing generations a standard type or breed can be developed and maintained. This rather sophisticated approach was seldom followed by the ancients and indeed it was almost unheard of until quite recently. Usually it was local conditions and temporary requirements that shaped the local horse without the aid of a considered breeding programme. When superior foreign horses were introduced to an area they were bred either indiscriminately by running them loose with the local animals, or used simply to produce a few exceptional offspring without thought of founding a breed. However almost

59

by chance some breeds were formed at an early period in history and the Arab horse is a case in point.

Before the Christian era Arabia was a strange remote land. Herodotus speaks of it as the home of the phoenix and of winged snakes that flew to Egypt each spring but gives no hint that there are horses of any kind in Arabia, only camels, asses and onagers. In the great army of Xerxes, the Arab contingent rode swift camels that were always kept well away from the cavalry to avoid upsetting the horses with their smell. Clearly the Arabs of that period were not thought of as horsemen at all, only as cameleers.

Anderson says that there is no description of the Arab horse prior to the sixth century AD when Timotheus of Gaza included Arabs in his catalogue of the four-footed beasts of the Middle East:

> Horses of good size, generally red-bay in colour, carrying their necks high, their faces regular and well-proportioned, carrying their heads close to their riders' faces, haughty and spirited, having superabundant pride, very keen, swift, with supple limbs, giving themselves wholly to the ardour of the course, bounding lightly rather than galloping, with compact flanks and lean bodies. The Arab horse is unwearied in the heat, rather rejoicing in the sun; his coat is beautiful, his diet simple, his bearing dignified.

Ridgeway [48] likewise considers that the Arabs were breeding horses by the sixth century for in that period a bitter tribal war is recorded as having been fought over the ownership of a certain famous animal named Dahis. However horses continued to be in scarce supply in the Arabian peninsula for another hundred years.

By then the armies of Islam had started the series of conquests that resulted, among other things, in bringing under their control all the major horse-producing countries of the Middle East and North Africa. Their first raid into Palestine and Iraq proved so easy and successful that they went on to subdue Syria, Turkey, Persia, Mesopotamia, Turkestan, Egypt and much of North Africa. Fisher [20] suggests that the Arabs did not set out with any clear-cut scheme for the conquest of the world and the extension of the Muslim faith, rather they made their empire as other states have made empires after them, blindly, with no objective other than plunder. It is a fair surmise that horses were a highly valued part of the loot. They would have been needed both to remount the Arab cavalry in the field and to reinforce the breeding stock at home, particularly in the Arabian peninsula itself which, as compared with the rest of the Middle East, was in its infancy so far as horse breeding was concerned.

Sealed off by its deserts and general remoteness from the world, Arabia was spared much of the turmoil and invasion that kept both the human and the equine populations of Eurasia in such a constant state of flux. In its happy isolation the country was free to evolve its own breeds of horse from the seventh century until almost the present day. Of course, in a country of this size there was bound to be some diversity in the stamp of animal produced by the various horse-breeding tribes, which often lived hundreds of miles apart. Strong views were expressed as to which tribe and which part of Arabia produced the best horses and, while good Arab horses were to be found in Syria, Iraq, Iran and Jordan, it was generally agreed that those horses bred in Nejd, the central plateau of the peninsula, were the best. That is to say of the best and purest lineage and the best fitted to endure the hardships of hunger, thirst and fatigue during distant forays into the desert to plunder rich caravans or to settle by force of arms some difference of opinion with a rival tribe. The desert was a wonderful testing ground for soundness of constitution and ability to survive under conditions of extreme privation. When a tribe's wealth, honour and very existence could depend on the prowess of its horses, selection of animals for breeding had to be based largely on surviving this grim test of performance; good looks and elegance of limbs and action were of very secondary importance.

However great, perhaps exaggerated, importance was attached to pedigree, which was always traced through the female line, back many generations to some famous foundation mare owned by a sheikh or tribe. It is remarkable that authentic breeding records could be maintained continuously by an illiterate people but lineage was a matter of deep concern to the Bedouin, as Carsten Niebuhr, the eighteenth-century traveller, explained in his memoirs:

The Arabians have indeed no tables of genealogy to prove the descent of their horses; yet they are sure of the legitimacy of the progeny; for a mare of this race is never covered unless in the presence of witnesses who must be Arabians. This people do not indeed always stickle at perjury; but in a case of such serious importance they are careful to deal conscientiously. There is no instance of false testimony given in respect to the descent of a horse. Every Arabian is persuaded that himself and his whole family would be ruined if he should prevaricate in giving his oath in an affair of such consequence. The Arabs make no scruples of selling their stallions but they are unwilling to part with their mares for money. When not in a condition to support them, they dispose of them to others on the terms of having a share in the foals, or of being at liberty to recover them after a certain time.

This highly selective breeding system practised over many generations created a hardy courageous animal well suited both to the military requirement for light cavalry as well as to the civilian demand in India and elsewhere for a small horse for riding and racing. As a result, during the nineteenth century the horse trade with the outside world reached such a height that the deserts were virtually stripped bare of their stock to meet the demand. Finally in the twentieth century with the onset of mechanization and the reduced opportunities for engaging in highwayman-like attacks on caravans and similar enterprises, horse breeding ceased to have much purpose for the Bedouin tribes and the true desert-bred horse has become almost a thing of the past. Nevertheless the sheer beauty of the Arab is immensely attractive to many people and perhaps because of this, as much as for any utilitarian purpose, admirers of the breed have set up Arab studs in a number of countries; in the Middle East, Europe, the Americas, South Africa, Australia and Japan. This wide dispersion is already creating new strains of the breed, a process that is hastened by the absence of an internationally recognized uniform definition of a pure-bred Arab, each country adhering to its own standards quite as fanatically as the different tribes of the Bedouin horse breeders of old.

The real importance of the Arab is not so much the utility and beauty of the breed but the extraordinarily effective part it has played in the upgrading and improvement of native stock all over the world and in the creation of new breeds. The English thoroughbred, for instance, is descended in part from the Arab and there can be few other breeds that do not show an Arab somewhere in their ancestry.

Officially the English thoroughbred dates from 1793 when the General Stud Book came into being. And from the foundation stock entered in the first volume, three direct male lines and some thirty direct female lines are still in existence at the present day. These ancestors were chiefly of oriental origin though some of the mares were of English or mixed English and oriental descent.

This historic landmark was preceded by several hundred years of growth of horse-racing and of racehorse breeding linked with the importation of foreign breeds. For instance in the sixteenth century any racehorse was likely to be called a Barbary horse if it had the least hint of foreign blood regardless of whether that came from Spain, Italy, Africa or Arabia; while animals of authentic eastern or African origin were often referred to quite indiscriminately as Turks, Arabs or Barbs, perhaps because all their homelands were contained within the Ottoman empire.

By the eighteenth century, as a result of many years of experience in cross-breeding with imported animals, it was common knowledge in England that the eastern horses nicked well with the native sort, producing offspring that were bigger and faster than either parent and for this and other reasons the introduction of breeding stock from abroad became fashionable and profitable.

The three foundation sires whose lines still survive all came from abroad, none of them was tried out on the racecourse and two of them, the Byerley Turk and the Godolphin Barb, came to England more by bizarre accident than by design.

The Byerley Turk is reputed to have been an animal of Arab breeding acquired by Captain Byerley as part of his share of the enormous booty seized from the Turks when their army was defeated and turned back from the gates of Vienna in 1683. Later, in 1690, Byerley used the horse as his charger when fighting for King William III at the battle of the Boyne in Ireland. Soon afterwards he and his charger retired to Yorkshire and to a more settled existence. From the Byerley Turk line came the famous racehorses Herod and The Tetrarch.

The Godolphin Barb, sometimes called the Godolphin Arabian, had an even stranger history. Some authors describe him as an ugly little horse with lop-ears and a vile temper. However his portrait by John Wooton, later copied by Stubbs, is more flattering than the written descriptions. He was one of a batch of eight Barbs presented to King Louis XV of France by the Bey of Tunis but, so the story goes, his meagre form and vicious behaviour did not endear him either to the king or to anyone else and he was passed rapidly from one new owner to another, finishing up dragging the heavy cart of a Parisian wood-merchant. From this hard labour he was rescued in 1729 by an English visitor, Edward Coke, who took him back to his stud in Derbyshire where he was known as the Paris Barb. A few years later, after Coke's death, the stallion was bought for Lord Godolphin's stud and given the name he bears today. The Godolphin line includes Matchem, Hurry On and the famous American horse Man O'War.

The third and perhaps the most influential male contributor to the development of the thoroughbred had a more conventional introduction to England. Thomas Darley, an English merchant living in Aleppo, in 1701 bought out of the Syrian desert a good-looking bay Arab colt of excellent pedigree which, in 1704, he shipped to his brother, who owned a stud in Yorkshire, sending with the animal a diffident note to the effect that he hoped the horse would not be too disliked in England. The Darley

Arabian, as he became known, quickly established his reputation as a sire of winners with such offspring as Whistlejacket and Flying Childers. Later in the line came Eclipse, St Simon and many other horses of outstanding merit.

The foundation, or tap-root mares as they are often referred to, appear to have been mostly Barbs, English and Barb-English crossed. True Arabian representation seems to have been small. There is no doubt that the Barb was one of the most important of the several strains that went into the making of the thoroughbred.

The Barb took its name from Barbary, that is the north-western corner of Africa that once included Morocco, Algeria and Tunis, plus Tangier, the Mediterranean port that Catherine Mary of Portugal brought as part of her dowry when she wedded King Charles II of England in 1662. At around this period, Barbary had a large and flourishing horse trade with Europe, exporting considerable numbers of horses annually to Spain and France in particular. Many of these animals were of indifferent quality but there were also plenty of good well-bred horses to be found among the shipments abroad and on the whole the Barb was prized as a racehorse, as an excellent light-cavalry mount and as a reliable sire for the improvement of other breeds. It was appreciated that one of the best breeds of light horse in Europe, the Andalusian, owed its excellence to Barb ancestry. And it was mainly horses of Andalusian descent that had recolonized America during the previous century.

Somewhat similar to the Arab in build, though differing from it in having a plainer head and lower set tail, the Barb usefully combined speed and endurance or, as one seventeenth-century author put it, 'when he is wakened and rode upon his mettle no horse is more nimble, vigorous and adroit and better for an Action of one or two hours. He makes a good stallion to breed Running Horses, the colts he gets being generally well-winded, fleet and good at bottom.'

In the years that followed, a number of factors led to the gradual deterioration of the breed. Youatt [66], writing in the early part of the nineteenth century, thought that the main reason was a long period of oppressive government that made it futile and unrewarding to attempt to raise good horses:

It is only among the tribes of the Desert, who are beyond the reach of the tyrants of their country, that the Barb of superior breed, and form, and power is to be found. Deep in the Sahara Desert is a noble breed of Barbs, known by the name of the Wind-Sucker or the Desert-horse. Jackson says of him that the

Desert-horse is to the common Barbary horse what the Desert-camel is to the usual camel of burden; but that he can only be induced to eat barley or wheat—oats are never given to horses in Africa; but that, supplied with a little camel's milk, he will travel almost incredible distances across the Desert. He is principally employed in hunting the antelope and the ostrich.

Since those days there has been a great deal of indiscriminate introduction of European and Arab blood and true Barbs have become a rarity, even in the desert.

Once the blend of Barb, Arab and English strains had become firmly established in England and the new breed, the thoroughbred, had proved its pre-eminence over any other sort of horse on the racecourse, it was only to be expected that other countries would import thoroughbreds and become competitive in the breeding of them. In fact both thoroughbred breeding and racing have become increasingly international in character. America, France and Italy especially have been very successful in developing their own bloodstock industries with animals descended mostly from ancestors registered in the English General Stud Book. The United States maintains its own register, the American Stud Book, but nevertheless, in common with the rest of the world, the United States regularly replenishes its studs with bloodstock from Britain.

Racecourse performance is not the only attribute of the thoroughbred. Two hundred years of intensive breeding has created a very prepotent animal, that is to say one capable of stamping its offspring with many of its own good qualities and desirable characteristics, and therefore most useful for the development and improvement of other breeds. For instance in England and Ireland the time-honoured formula for producing a hunter is to mate a thoroughbred stallion with a mare of a heavier type. Ideally the offspring combines the weight-carrying ability of the dam with the elegance, spirit and athleticism of the sire.

Incidentally a large proportion of the mounts of the Household Cavalry, both the blacks of the troopers and the greys of the trumpeters, are Irish-bred animals of the hunter type. Some have the carriage and elegance denoting a high proportion of thoroughbred blood, others incline more to the sturdiness and placidity of their dams; and, for ceremonial duties in London, a strong quiet half-bred with a comfortable action is often preferable to a spirited thoroughbred which may have little patience with crowds and traffic. The quietest and strongest ceremonial horses, those carrying the drums, seldom possess any thoroughbred blood. These huge, skewbald or piebald animals, standing seventeen hands or more, are not allowed out of a walk with their weighty unwieldy loads, and their riders, who must have both hands free for the drum sticks, guide them by means of reins attached to the stirrups. Other hunter-type animals to be seen on the streets of London include the horses of the Mounted Police and the gun teams of the King's Troop, Royal Horse Artillery.

Another interesting cross, that of Arab horse with thoroughbred mare, has been developed into a new breed, the Anglo-Arab, which happily combines the greater size and speed of the English strain with the grace and gaiety of the Arabian, producing very often a lovely show or dressage horse with a good cross-country performance. The thoroughbred has also been used to improve the size and appearance of many of the British breeds of pony. For example, Marsk, the sire of the great Eclipse, ran out with the New Forest ponies 1765–9. Valuable show ponies and excellent small hunters are produced by the introduction of thoroughbred blood but at the risk of losing the natural hardiness and frugality of the native breeds that have been accustomed for generations to a semi-feral existence on hill and moorland.

It is quite instructive to compare the pretty little show ponies and miniature hunters of today with an expert's description of their ancestors a hundred and fifty years ago. Youatt [66] writes as follows of the ponies he knew in the early nineteenth century.

The modern New Foresters, notwithstanding their Marsk blood, are generally ill-made, large-headed, short-necked, and ragged-hipped; but hardy, safe and useful, with much of their ancient spirit and speed, and all their old paces. The catching of these ponies is as great a trial of skill as the hunting of the wild horse on the Pampas of South America, and a greater one of patience.

The Welsh pony is one of the most beautiful little animals that can be imagined. He has a small head, high withers, deep yet round barrel, short joints, flat legs and good round feet. He will live on any fare and will never tire.

The Exmoor ponies, although ugly enough, are hardy and useful. A well-known sportsman says he rode one of them half-a-dozen miles and never felt such power and action in so small a compass before.

There is on Dartmoor a race of ponies much in request in that vicinity, being sure-footed and hardy and admirably calculated to scramble over the rough roads and dreary wilds of that mountainous district. The Dartmoor pony is larger than the Exmoor and, if possible, uglier.

The Highland pony is far inferior to the Galloway. The head is large; he is low before, long in the back, short in the legs, upright in the pasterns, rather slow in his paces and not pleasant to ride except in the canter. His habits make him hardy, for he is rarely housed in the summer or the winter. When these

66

animals come to any boggy piece of ground, they first put their nose to it and then pat it a peculiar way with one of their forefeet; and from the sound and feel of the ground they know whether it will bear them. They do the same with ice, and determine in a minute whether they will proceed.

The Shetland pony, called in Scotland 'sheltie', an inhabitant of the extreme northern Scottish isles, is a very diminutive animal—sometimes not more than seven and a half hands in height, and rarely exceeding nine and a half. He is often exceedingly beautiful with a small head, good-tempered countenance, a short neck, fine towards the throttle, shoulders low and thick—in so small a creature far from being a blemish—back short, quarters expanded and powerful, legs flat and fine, and pretty round feet. These ponies possess immense strength for their size; will fatten upon almost anything; and are perfectly docile. One of them nine hands (or three feet) in height, carried a man of twelve stone forty miles in one day.

All these mountain and moorland breeds described by Youatt are in existence still and, along with the sturdy Connemara pony of Ireland and the Fell and Dales ponies of northern England, make excellent riding ponies; and when crossed with the thoroughbred or Arab, good show and hunter ponies can result.

Each breed has its stud book and one would say that on the whole the quality and standards of the breeds are well maintained and perhaps improved: even Youatt's critical eye might now view the Forest, Exmoor and Dartmoor ponies with favour. Height also has been improved on average, perhaps because of better care and feeding, and it is often a problem to keep well-nourished pony stock within the height limits of the breed. However diet may not be the sole cause of the phenomenon: the size of a foal is probably controlled more by maternal influence than by the amount of food given. Thus Walton and Hammond [64] have shown that in reciprocal crosses between the large Shire horse and the little Shetland pony the size of the foal follows the size of the dam. The internal secretions of the small Shetland dam limit the size of the foal to such as she can give birth to. On the other hand the cross-bred foal out of the Shire mare is three times as large at birth as the cross-bred foal out of the Shetland mare. At four years old the differences are still marked, the former being still one and a half times heavier than the latter.

The origins of the pony breeds are obscure. But when roads were either non-existent or so bad as to be impassable to wheeled traffic, pack ponies were the chief means of transporting goods of all varieties. Summerhays [57] says of the Fell pony that he was once used in great numbers to carry coal and lead from the mines to the coast for shipment. Sixteen stone of lead was carried by each animal and with this load these fourteen-hand ponies would travel in droves of twenty at a fast walk in charge of one mounted man, covering thirty miles and more each day.

In direct contrast to the ponies are the massive draught horses, such as the Shires, Clydesdales and Suffolk Punches of Britain and the Percherons of France. In the Middle Ages, heavy horses, or 'great horses' as they were called then, were bred specifically to carry the heavily armoured fighting men of the period and the supply never seems to have met the military requirement, which made them expensive to buy as well as being costly to keep adequately fed in proportion to their body size. From the civilian point of view they were uneconomic animals as compared with the smaller breeds and moreover they did not fit into the civilian transport system, which was based on saddle horses and pack ponies, or the farming practices of the day, which were geared to slow-moving teams of oxen.

A number of factors brought the heavy horses into general use, including the disappearance of iron-clad men from the battlefield, improvements in roads and vehicles, which encouraged the use of coaches and carts, and the development of new agricultural practices and machinery which rendered ox-haulage obsolete on the land. By the seventeenth and eighteenth centuries definite local types were emerging: the general purpose Yorkshire horse, the huge sluggish black horse of the Midlands and the more active Suffolk Punch of East Anglia, as well as a great many heavy horses of indeterminate breed reared to meet the insatiable demand for such animals in town and country; for this was a time of considerable population growth and industrial expansion and harness horses were as essential then to the quickening tempo of life as the steam-engine and the internal-combustion engine in later eras.

The pioneer of animal breeding, Robert Bakewell, included the English black horse in the species that he set out to improve and from it, by a process of careful selection, he created the Shire horse, which retained the size of the parent stock but without the torpidity that had led the black horse to being described as 'the snail breed better calculated for eating than working and whose tendency is to render their drivers as sluggish as themselves'. The breed has its own stud book and typical Shires, which may be black, bay or grey in colour, are around seventeen hands in height and may weigh a ton or more. Their size, weight and activity enable them to shift enormous loads and this capability coupled with their good looks and great presence ensures their continuing popularity as work horses in Britain and in many other countries.

In Scotland, the developing demand for cart-horses was met by the judicious mating of imported Flemish stallions to the old packhorse type of mare that existed in the Clyde Valley at the end of the eighteenth century. Shire blood was also introduced but the Clydesdale has been a distinctive breed from at least 1878 when the first volume of the Clydesdale Stud Book was published. The Clydesdale is built on less massive lines than the Shire but it possesses a combination of muscular strength and agility that makes it a valuable draught animal. The coat colour may be bay, brown or black, with a lot of white on the face and legs.

In France, the farmers of the province of La Perche in Normandy founded the most widespread and popular of the heavy breeds, the Percheron, by combining a little eastern blood with that of several of the continental and English breeds of draught horse. The Percheron is a very strong, short-legged active horse, grey or black in colour. As well as in France, it has been bred extensively in Britain, the United States and Canada. At one time about ninety per cent of the London bus horses were American-bred Percherons and in the First World War the British Army made great use of the Percheron for pulling its heavy artillery.

The Suffolk Punch, as its name indicates, is a powerful chunky animal and of great courage. Youatt [66] says of him: 'The Suffolk would tug at a dead pull until he dropped. It was beautiful to see a team of true Suffolks at a signal from the driver and without the whip, down on their knees in a moment, and drag everything before them. Brutal wagers were frequently laid as to their power in this respect, and many a good team was injured and ruined. The immense power of the Suffolk is accounted for by the low position of the shoulder which enables him to throw so much weight into his collar.' All Suffolks trace back in the male line to one stallion foaled in 1760, and the purity of the line may be gauged from the fact that all Suffolks are chestnut in colour.

The Cleveland Bay was another breed created to meet the demand for specialized types of harness horse. The breed originated from the sturdy pack ponies of the itinerant chapmen, who once peddled their wares across the Yorkshire moors. At first the ponies were crossed with heavy horses as strength rather than speed was needed to haul the cumbersome coaches of the eighteenth century. Then, as coach design improved thoroughbred blood was introduced, creating a fast powerful animal that was in great demand for both the stage-coach and the private carriage trade. The first volume of the Cleveland Bay Stud Book was published in 1884, since when no extraneous blood has been admitted. The Cleveland Bay is a general purpose 'ride or drive' type of horse resembling a rather long-backed heavy-weight hunter. The colour is, of course, always bay with black points; the only white permitted is in the form of a small star on the forehead. Very good hunters can result from crossing the Cleveland Bay with the thoroughbred.

In America most of the European and eastern breeds of horse have been tried out at one time or another since the seventeenth century, and some, such as the thoroughbred, have become established as American varieties of the original strains. Also available in the earlier days on the western plains were the semi-wild mustangs of Spanish origin that provided mounts for Indian and cow-hand alike. From the wealth of equine material at their disposal, Americans have blended many strains to form a number of special-purpose breeds including the Quarter Horse, the Standard Bred, the Morgan, the American Saddle Horse and the Tennessee Walking Horse.

The Quarter Horse was developed in Virginia towards the end of the eighteenth century by mating thoroughbred stallions to native mares of Spanish blood. The cross produced a very versatile agile type of cob which, when it had completed all the chores on the farm, could show a fine turn of speed on the improvised quarter-mile race tracks then in vogue, earning its first title 'The Famous and Celebrated Colonial Quarter Pather'. Later its nimbleness led to its adoption by ranchers as the ideal cow-pony and today it is the most popular riding horse in the United States.

The Standard Bred trotters and pacers show the same courage and attain almost the same speed at those gaits as their thoroughbred ancestors did at a gallop. They are bred and used for harness racing and their name dates from 1879 when the National Association of Trotting Horse Breeders ruled that a trotter for admission to the register must be able to cover a measured mile within a standard time, a time that today is set at two minutes twenty seconds.

The Morgan traces back in the male line to a single stallion, named Justin Morgan after his owner, which was foaled in 1793 and is believed to have been of thoroughbred parentage. He was a tough little horse of between fourteen and fifteen hands and, considering his size, his stamina, strength and speed were quite extraordinary. He was a very prepotent sire and transmitted his good qualities to his offspring, thus founding a remark-ably useful breed of general-purpose horse.

The American Saddle Horse is a blend of a number of breeds of light horse, including the thoroughbred and the Morgan. In addition to the natural walk, trot and canter, some Saddle Horses are trained to two artificial movements, the slow-gait, which is a sort of prancing walk; and the rack, which is a similar movement carried out in fast time. The modern Saddle Horse is essentially an elegant show animal but originally the breed was created with the very practical purpose of producing the perfect riding horse for comfortable long-distance travel.

The Tennessee Walking Horse or the Plantation Walking Horse was developed on very similar lines to the Saddle Horse and for much the same purpose, that is, to provide an easy ride for men who had to spend many hours in the saddle. The breed's particular attribute is a smooth fast-running walk, which takes both horse and rider over the ground with the minimum of effort and fatigue.

Chapter 12

Some Breeds of the Soviet Union

WITHIN living memory herds of wild horses roamed free on the Eurasian steppes, as their ancestors had done for thousands of years, and there is good evidence that this part of the world was the original home of *Equus caballus* and the area where the species was first brought into the service of man. But the Soviet Union covers a sizeable portion of the earth's surface, with many different types of terrain and a number of markedly different climatic zones, each with its own distinctive flora and fauna. It is not surprising therefore that during several thousand years of domestication over thirty distinct varieties of horse should have developed in the Soviet Union, shaped by their environment and the requirements of their human owners.

For instance in the coniferous forests of the far north, verging on the arctic circle, are to be found the woolly-coated fat-padded horses that for centuries have played a vital role in the transport and lumbering operations of those regions of deep snow and intense cold; two thousand miles to the south, in the arid deserts and uplands of central Asia, are the lean, thin-coated, speedy horses, which once carried the Turkoman warriors on their raids into Persia, and which the Chinese once coveted so greatly because of their superior and celestial qualities; and, on the prairie-like steppes, the hardy indestructible ponies, which time and again have carried invading nomad hordes into Europe and China. Inevitably there has been much casual unplanned mingling of the different equine strains. Also many deliberate measures have been taken to improve the native breeds and to create useful new varieties by one means or another, including the importation of foreign blood.

A typical example of successful upgrading with imported stock can be seen in the Don Horse, one of the best of the Russian saddle-horses. Its ancestors, the mounts of the Cossack cavalry that, in 1812, harried so unmercifully Napoleon's grand army in its retreat from Moscow, were tough ugly ponies, excellent for this sort of guerrilla action but too small for the effective use of regular cavalry. During the latter half of the nineteenth century, Persian, Arab and thoroughbred stallions were introduced into the Don breeding herds and kept with them for a period of years until the cross-bred stock, relatively large animals of around sixteen hands, were considered to be breeding true to type, combining the size of the foreign sires with the hardiness of the indigenous dams. As of old, the new improved Don breed is reared on the open steppes around the Don and Volga rivers under the traditional *taboune* system in which about a hundred and twenty mares are run out with six or so stallions, each stallion forming his own group or *kossiacky* of about twenty mares. A foaling rate of about ninety per cent is said to be quite usual under this semi-feral system of management, which mimics to some extent the grouping of a true wild herd until weaning time. Then at the age of ten or eleven months, the young stock are separated from their dams and grazed on another section of the steppe until they have become sufficiently mature to be caught up for training and work.

From the Don another breed has been developed, called the Anglo-Don or Budenny. Originally the intention was to produce for military purposes a bigger faster animal than the Don by infusing still more thoroughbred blood into the breed, and it is of interest that the Cossack corps of the German army had a number of these good-looking animals in its ranks when it surrendered to the British forces in Austria in 1945. Nowadays the Anglo-Don competes successfully in steeplechases and in every sort of equestrian field event.

Another handsome breed, the Strelets, was evolved during the nineteenth century by the Strelets State Stud, situated in the Ukrainian steppes, by mating several indigenous breeds with the Arab. The resulting Russian-Arab was similar in appearance and characteristics to the Anglo-Arab but before the breed had a chance to prove itself, it was virtually extinguished during the First World War. The Strelets breed, or something very similar, is now being resurrected in several north Caucasian studs under the name of the Tersk horse. The Tersk horses resemble rather robust Arabs. Mostly light-grey in colour, they are popular as saddle-horses and their elegance and placidity make them ideal performers in the circus ring.

For the horses of central Asia Youatt [66] has a kind if critical word:

Turkistan is that part of South Tartary north-east of the Caspian Sea and has been celebrated from very early times for producing a pure and valuable breed

73

of horses. They are called *Toorkomans*. They are said to be preferable even to the pure Persian for actual service. They are large, from 15 to 16 hands high, swift and inexhaustible under fatigue. Some of them have travelled nine hundred miles in eleven successive days. They are however somewhat too small in the barrel, too long on the legs, occasionally ewe-necked, and always having a head out of proportion large: yet such are the good qualities of the horse, that one of pure blood is worth two or three hundred pounds even in that country.

Two notable modern breeds have been derived from these animals: the Akhal-Teke and the Jomud. Barmintsev [6], the director of the Moscow All-Union Research Institute of Horse-Breeding, says that the Akhal-Teke is unique on several counts: because of the antiquity of the breed and its ability to work effectively under even the most extreme desert conditions, and because of the peculiar management it is subjected to; by this he means that owing to the absence of natural grazing in those regions, the Turkmans, instead of running them free like the ponies of the steppe, keep their horses tethered, feeding them on a light but highly nutritious diet of pelleted food consisting of mutton fat, barley and alfalfa and, when at rest, covering them with blankets to preserve the metallic sheen of their fine silky coats, a much admired feature of the breed.

The closely related Jomud is a smaller animal, somewhat similar in conformation to the Arab. It is reared and kept under more natural conditions than the Akhal-Teke but, like the Akhal-Teke, the Jomud is trained to endure thirst and all the other hardships of desert life. Representatives of both these breeds once took part in a ride of nearly 3000 miles, from Ashkabad to Moscow; 225 miles of this journey was through the Kara Kum desert and despite only a few mouthfuls of water being available the horses covered this distance in three days without apparent harm.

An interesting type of horse, adapted to the very different climatic conditions of the Urals, is the Bashkir. The males of this breed are used mostly for general transport purposes such as riding or for pulling sleighs, and Bashkir troikas are expected to average seventy-five miles a day over the snow. The mares, on the other hand, are kept mainly for their milk, producing about two gallons daily, from which the slightly alcoholic drink *kumiss* is prepared by a fermentative process. In fact in many parts of Russia the old nomad practice persists of relying on the horse for meat and milk, and other necessities of life as well as for riding and haulage. For example the Kazakh horses are used for cattle-herding work on the steppes of Kazakhastan but these stout little animals are also valued for the meat and milk they provide for human consumption. And, in the northern territories, the strong shaggy-coated Yakut horse is a general utility animal not only because it is used for riding, pack and harness purposes but because it also provides meat and milk. And its thick coat not only protects the animal from the bitter winter cold and the agonizing attacks of the summer insect swarms: it also provides hair and wool for weaving.

Barmintsev [6] says:

The Yakut horse is one of the most remarkable breeds in the world. The Yakut's territory, which extends far beyond the polar circle, includes some of the coldest areas of the Northern Hemisphere, the average winter temperature being minus 40 to 50 degrees centigrade. Yakut horses graze on grasslands in the valleys of the Lena, Yana and Kal'na rivers and also on the taiga glades, and dig out their food from under deep snow. No less stamina is required of Yakuts during the brief summer, then the animals are attacked by myriads of blood-sucking insects.

Sport has also played a large part in the development of breeds. In central Asia, the Karabair horses of Samarkand and the Lokai horses of the Pamir owe much of the thought and care devoted to the improvement of their speed, courage and agility to the local passion for the hard and dangerous game of *Kok-par*. In this contest rival factions of mounted men battle for the possession of the carcase of a goat and then fight to carry the trophy triumphantly through the goal. In Uzbetkistan, good *Kok-par* horses are almost as costly as good polo ponies in this country.

But fast trotting races were the sport that appealed most to the Russian people. Hayes [28], who was employed towards the end of the nineteenth century by the Russian minister of war at the Russian army remount depots and in St Petersburg, says that the wealthier Russians loved to go as fast as their coachmen could drive them, even over the roughest cobble-stone pavements. He goes on to say:

match-trotting is greatly patronised by the Russian public, who, in St. Petersburg, assemble in the stands of the famous trotting ground of the Semenovsky Platz in large crowds, every Sunday and on other occasions throughout the winter, to witness the races that are run there. Some of the match-trotters are very fast from the European point of view and have got inside two minutes twenty seconds for the mile. Russian trotting men are bitterly jealous of the American professionals who have settled in their midst, and who make a good living out of the game. For this, the Americans deserve a great deal of credit. Almost all the horses which compete in these races have been bred in Russia and show more or less admixture of American and English blood.

75

The formation of a distinct breed of Russian harness horse dates back to the eighteenth century when agriculture was being greatly expanded and improved farming methods, such as deep ploughing of the soil, were being introduced; these factors no doubt created a demand for a bigger more active type of farm horse. Also at this period the empty distant land of Siberia was being colonized and brought under cultivation, and the need for strong fast horses for intercommunication would have been obvious to a man of intelligence like Count Alexei Orlov, the ablest of the extraordinary Orlov brothers, who dethroned their sovereign, Peter III, in favour of his queen, Catherine, later to be called Catherine the Great. For many years the brothers enjoyed a privileged position at court, enhanced by the Queen taking the elder brother, Gregory, as her official lover and chief counsellor. This happy state of affairs ended when Catherine took Prince Potemkin into her bed and confidence. Alexei was a violent man: he had probably seen personally to the killing of Peter III, and he avenged the family honour by thrashing Potemkin and knocking out one of his eyes, before withdrawing from court to the huge Orlov estate to the south of Moscow, where he spent the next thirty-five years in horse-breeding operations that were mainly directed to the development of a fast-trotting general-purpose harness horse, the Orlov Trotter.

The founding sire of the Orlov Trotter breed was the grey Arab stallion, Smetanka, which was imported from Greece in 1775 and mated to Dutch cart-mares. To the Arab-Dutch cross was added thoroughbred, Danish, Persian and other foreign blood until a fairly standard type of animal was evolved, fast enough for carriages, troikas and racing sleighs and substantial enough for more everyday duties. Rather typically, Count Alexei never allowed any of his breeding stock out of his possession. He died in 1808, bequeathing his studs, five million roubles and thirty thousand serfs to his daughter. She continued her father's policies until 1845 when she sold the stud to the government and permitted Orlov stallions and Orlov broodmares to be dispersed throughout the country to other breeding centres. It has become one of the most famous breeds in Russia.

Among the breeds that have been developed from the Orlov Trotter are the Russian Trotter, obtained by adding American Trotter and thoroughbred blood to the Orlov strain; the Russian Heavy Draught Horse derived from a mixture of Orlov, indigenous cart-horses, Percheron and Ardenne blood; and the Toric Draught Horse of Estonia, which has evolved mainly from a cross between native Estonian horses and the Norfolk Trotter (a now-extinct breed of English roadster), with Orlov blood added so as to produce an active medium-weight animal capable of working both on the land and on the road.

On the whole the medium-sized animal is better suited to Russian agricultural conditions than the massive breeds of western Europe, which are considered to be too big for practical purposes, too expensive to feed and seldom capable of adapting satisfactorily to the severe winter climate. However one popular breed of very heavy draught horse has been evolved: the Vladimir. The Vladimir Heavy Draught Horse was developed by crossing indigenous cart-mares with Shire and Clydesdale stallions. In appearance it is a slightly smaller version of its British forebears but, nevertheless, it is an extremely powerful animal, combining speed with great pulling power.

Chapter 13

Social Behaviour

IT is customary among civilized peoples to think of horses as solitary individuals and, very often, to keep them in stables and loose-boxes where they are isolated from their fellows for most of the time. Despite many centuries of this type of treatment the domestic horse has retained the gregarious nature of its wild ancestors, and given the opportunity, horses will quickly revert to the herd existence that the species once enjoyed on the steppes and plains of Europe and Asia. Its behaviour frequently reminds one of this innate link with the past: its calm content while in the company of other horses and its noisy anxiety when separated from those familiar companions; the way a school horse, accustomed to being one of a troop, often needs strong persuasion before it will leave the comforting presence of its mates to be ridden out alone; or the way a nervous youngster will follow the lead of an older animal over an obstacle that had previously seemed insurmountable. Horses on the whole dislike a solitary life and it may well be that some of the aimless self-destructive habits known as stable vices, weaving and crib-biting for instance, are responses to the stress and frustration that a lonely existence imposes on animals, which in the natural state seldom moved out of sight of other members of the herd and lived in an environment where their social instincts had full play.

Good first-hand reports of the behaviour of wild-horse herds are rare and somewhat lacking in detail but the older descriptions coupled with the more recent observations made on mustangs and other feral horses suggest that the true ancient pattern of grouping of the wild horses had much in common with the way of life of the plains and mountain zebras of today. Luckily these species are still well represented in Africa, particularly the plains variety, the burchelline zebras, and they have been the subject of very detailed studies by Klingel [32].

The typical herd of plains zebras is simply a family made up of a stallion accompanied by one to six mares together with their foals, yearlings and a few older offspring. There are seldom more than sixteen animals in one of these groups and when larger herds than this do occur they are the result of numerous families being brought together by favourable grazing conditions, or perhaps by a seasonal migratory movement to better pastures; thousands of animals may then congregate together. When conditions change the families again drift apart.

The herd has a rank order: a system of precedence among its members, all of whom, as it were, know their place in the hierarchy and recognize one another by stripe pattern, voice and scent. This organization minimizes aggressive behaviour and fighting within the family. The stallion takes priority in feeding and drinking and is dominant in most other situations; then come the mares in order of age, size and truculence, then the young. When on the move, the senior mare is generally in the lead and the stallion brings up the rear or he may travel at the side of the herd. At other times, and more especially during the breeding season, the stallion moves constantly round his herd, keeping it together and challenging and chasing off potential rivals. Actually the mares and their young form a natural cohesive unit of themselves and they remain united whether or not the stallion is there. If he dies or leaves the herd for any reason, the normal family existence continues unchanged until, eventually, another male adopts the herd as his own; his entry into the family seems to be accepted as a matter of course by the females and colts alike and without disturbance of the rank relationships.

The young males leave their family groups between the ages of one to three years, not because they are driven away by the stallion as potential rivals; in fact they are usually on friendly terms with him, but more it would seem from a desire to consort and play with other colts. Bachelor herds are formed of about fifteen strong; these are loose associations of individuals among whom there is no apparent rank order. The bachelor herd is a fairly stable organization though, of course, colts will break away from time to time to form their own family units with any available fillies and mares that they may succeed in acquiring.

The young female as a rule leaves the family group at a rather younger age than her brother, often when only fifteen months old, at the time of her first oestrus. The early heat period is seldom fertile but the signs of heat are pronounced and extremely attractive to the roving young males, members of the bachelor herd. They are usually too numerous to be driven off by the family stallion, who may become utterly exhausted in his efforts

79

to chase them away, as there is little actual fighting. In the end, one male out of a dozen or more persistent males succeeds in abducting the filly, driving her away from her family. The attachment between the filly and her abductor is seldom permanent: she spends about a year consorting with one stallion or family group after another until she finally comes to maturity and settles down with the stallion she happens to be with at the time. If he already possesses a family group she becomes one of his harem; if he is a bachelor then she becomes the nucleus of a new herd.

Exact comparisons of this herd behaviour pattern with that shown by feral horses in America, Europe and Australia are hard to make because few of the feral herds escape interference from man to a greater or lesser degree. Indiscriminate hunting, round-ups, culling and so forth, all affect the composition of the herd and its way of life. However when horses have their full freedom for several generations, they do adopt the same social organization of family and bachelor groups as that used by the plains and mountain zebras – which is perhaps the basic social pattern for the genus *Equus*. An example can be found in the grouping of feral horses of Sable Island in the North Atlantic.

It seems that horses were shipped to this desolate little island from Massachusetts early in the eighteenth century. Crew and Buchanan Smith [14] quote local reports indicating that in 1864 there were 400 ponies running free there. They were organized into a number of herds, each with its own feeding area. The animals were described as being quite wild; the males were fierce and slept standing, seldom relaxing their vigilant guard of their herds. In size and appearance, with their heavy hairy heads and thick coats, the ponies were said to resemble the tarpan and the authors inferred that the very harsh environment acting over a period of one and a half centuries had moulded the form of these animals to something very similar to that of their remote ancestors. Tyler [62], quoting a 1967 report, states that these horses, still completely undisturbed by man, live in groups consisting of one stallion, a small number of mares and some of their off-spring in a manner that closely parallels the organization of the plains zebras, including the formation of the surplus males into bachelor herds.

Modifications of this social pattern have been noted by Tyler [62] in her detailed study of the semi-feral ponies of the New Forest. The New Forest, a former royal hunting reserve in southern England, covers 144 square miles of heath, woodland and bog and carries a pony population of about 2500. The mares for the most part live out their lives in the Forest;

foraging for themselves, mating, foaling and rearing their young up to the time of weaning without much interference from man, who exerts his influence by the culling of aged and unfit animals, by the sorting out of young stock for sale and by allowing only selected stallions to breed in the Forest. In annual round-ups the foals are caught and branded; most of the fillies are turned free again together with a select few of the colts that are judged suitable for breeding purposes. In all about 120 approved stallions are permitted to breed in the Forest, obviously only a fraction of the number of adult males that would be present in the natural state.

The shortage of males has a number of effects on the social organization of the Forest ponies. Thus many of the family groups consist of mares and their offspring only and the stallions each serve several groups, one of which may become, as it were, his home base for feeding and resting purposes. Another result of the male dearth is the absence of bachelor herds with a consequent decreased pressure on the fillies to break the strong parental ties at an early age, causing some Forest fillies to remain with their dams until four years of age; and, on leaving their families the fillies at first tend to attach themselves temporarily to one group of mares after another instead of adopting the more heterosexual approach to adolescent life of the zebras.

It is common knowledge among horsemen that horses have a good directional sense that can guide them back to their stables from considerable distances. Tyler [62] found numerous instances of this homing ability among Forest ponies and she quotes instances of ponies being removed from the Forest, sometimes by motor horse-box, and finding their way back to their old home ranges, over a period of two or three days, from points of release twelve or so miles away. Hafez [25] considers that the recognition of the home range depends largely on the sense of smell, probably the smell of excreta. He states that in some experiments carried out to determine the factors involved in homing, it was noted that there was a strong tendency for unguided horses in strange surroundings to walk up-wind. When the wind was blowing from the homeward direction homing was far more evident than at other times.

Normally animals seldom stray from their home range so long as it provides the basic requirements of their existence: food, water, shelter from high winds and storms, and, in summer, protective shade from the sun and from the attacks of insect pests; also the sense of security derived from living in a familiar environment with the family group. The home ranges of the different groups freely overlap, grazing areas and resting places are shared peaceably and there is no sign of any true marked-out territories, which one group would defend against another.

Among equids, the only species to show definite territorial behaviour is Grevy's zebra, mainly a desert species, and the male does mark out a territory with his dung and urine during the breeding season. He drives his mares into this area and vigorously resists any attempt by rival males to encroach on his territory. For the rest of the year there is a tendency for males and females to live apart.

Antonius [4] asserts that in the African wild ass the sexes also remain separate for most of the year. Possibly because of this estrangement between the sexes, the male and female take a very hostile attitude towards each other when they meet for the first time during the mating season and indulge in a great deal of vicious fighting. Inter-male rivalry is therefore minimal, all the stallions' energies being needed to subdue their mares, leaving neither time nor strength for less vital activities. It has been suggested that fighting is an essential part of the courtship ritual of the wild ass and that the female has to be chased, bitten and kicked before she can become fully receptive to the male. Leading on from this idea, Antonius wonders whether it could be an explanation of why the mating of the jack-ass and the mare is easier to achieve than the reciprocal cross of the horse with the jenny-ass: perhaps, he suggests, to the male ass the mare is merely an unusually compliant female; whereas the female ass needs a fight to release her sexual responses and is therefore unable to accept the stallion's normal peaceful services. However it must be said that the domestic jenny-ass here in Britain usually manages very well without such painful preliminaries, though, of course, any equid female that is not fully in season will probably resist male approaches quite violently. Any difficulties encountered in the mating of horse and ass are more likely to be due to inadequate time and thought having been given to overcoming, by sensible conditioning procedures, the natural aversion that one species may have to mating with another.

The equid males possess a strong herding instinct towards their mares, which they will drive together and defend from other males. The possessiveness of the male of the majority of the species is centred on their herds, which must be defended wherever they may be and not, as in the case of Grevy's zebra, only when it is within a marked territory. In the true horses under natural conditions, mares and stallions remain together throughout the year. But when, as in the New Forest, males are in short supply the members of the harems of the various stallions drift apart at the end of the mating season and split up into the individual family groups of mares and offspring which have already been described.

With the gestation period of the equids varying from eleven months in the horse to slightly over a year in other species, the breeding and foaling seasons inevitably overlap. These seasons occur during the spring and summer, that is when the hours of daylight are increasing. Single births are the rule as the equid uterus is seldom successful in supporting the life of two foetuses; and even if twins are born they are often small and weakly. The act of birth is generally a quick and easy affair and the foal is on its feet within an hour or so, when it will begin to suck.

Immediately after birth, while wet with foetal fluids and still too weak to stand, the horse foal is vigorously licked by its mother. This attention is clearly important not only in drying the young creature but also in establishing a firm maternal link with it. Probably mostly by her sense of smell, the mare knows in future that that is her foal and she will usually refuse to allow any other foal to suck from her or even to come near her. Tyler [62] observed that the Forest pony foals, once they were on their feet, would during their first day of life follow any large moving object, whether their mother, other mares, humans, or even, in one case, a motor van. She describes one foal that showed a marked attachment to one particular tree, refusing to leave it to follow the mother when she moved away. In the New Forest it is apparently accepted that foals will at times attempt to suck from a tree, totally ignoring their mothers who will eventually desert them. The Van Lawick-Goodalls [63] have reported an instance of a similar type of behaviour in a zebra foal. These are merely anecdotes, but in other mammals imprinting, a rapid form of learning at a very early age, is well proven. Harrison Matthews [27] observes amusingly enough that the phenomenon is described in the nursery rhyme of 'Mary and her little lamb'. The lamb that went wherever Mary went is a typical example of mal-imprinting, the process by which the young of many wild animals can be tamed and brought to tolerate captivity; breeding from such animals is likely to be difficult because they have identified themselves so completely with man that their own species has ceased to have any social significance for them.

Not all foals that fail to suck are victims of mal-imprinting. More probably they have suffered brain damage through some accident during birth, which makes them incapable of reacting normally; the so-called 'dummy foals' that have no sucking reflex cannot recognize their mothers. But Glendinning and Williams [23 and 65] have shown that the hand-rearing of orphan foals in isolation can produce abnormal behaviour. The hand-reared foal adopts the human handler as its mother and becomes unable to understand or relate normally to other horses; and because of its lack of common sense it may be difficult to train in later life. On the other hand animals that are not accustomed to man early in life are apt to be shy and wild. The training of horses handled from birth is usually a simple education, provided that they have had normal social contacts with their own kind. Conversely the training of animals allowed to run wild until maturity is very often a harsh and relatively ineffective process of breaking the will to resist discipline. Obviously for successful domestication, young animals should be accustomed to man as early as possible in life in a quiet unobtrusive way that does not alienate them from their own kind. Orphaned foals should have the company of other horses; or, failing this, a sheep, goat, calf, or donkey, seem reasonably effective substitutes. Glendinning [23] says that on different occasions she has found that two baby yaks and a baby llama served the same purpose well; perhaps this was merely because they prevented boredom and provided competition at feeding time. Similarly, a goat may be used to provide company and distraction for a solitary adult horse: often in the belief that its example will prevent its companion panicking should the stable catch fire; or, with a brood-mare, because it is hoped that the calming caprine presence will eliminate any possibility of the occurrence of abortion.

Foals will nibble at grass in the first few days of life, though there are indications that they start to graze properly through imitating the movements of their dams. In much the same way the other characteristic equine behaviour patterns are released, such as rolling, stamping, scratching and shaking; also mutual grooming, the mare and foal nibbling at one another's manes and bodies: a companionable social habit that is carried on throughout life with selected grooming partners. During its first week the foal sucks from its mother about four times an hour and then with decreasing frequency until it ceases altogether at the age of about one year as a rule, when the dam is within a few days of giving birth to a new foal.

Throughout the suckling period the foal is developing its behaviour in relation to the rest of the herd. In its early days the dam stays close by, threatening other animals, including man, that come too close and heading off the foal from any dangerously inquisitive approach to other mares or to stallions. These are rarely aggressive to foals but occasionally some particularly dominant female may make a savage attack and, during the mating season, stallions have been known to maul and kill young foals.

Before the end of the first month the foal starts to spend more time away from the side of its dam, largely galloping, romping and grooming with other foals of both sexes of its own age. Later as the colts get rougher in their play and indulge in mock-fights, there tends to be a separation of colts and fillies though precocious sexual behaviour, such as mounting of one by the other, also occurs.

Play is obviously an enjoyable experience, a matter of fun and high spirits. But as the young indulge their exuberance, they are in fact also rehearsing with their fellows all the types of skill and behaviour that are basic to equine life; and learning to use the code of communication that serves to order the existence of their species. Ideally these play-experiences reinforce and add to those received through the care and example of the mother. However as mentioned previously, in the case of orphans, play with other young animals can to some extent compensate for deprivation of maternal contact. Ewer [19] quotes observations on the behaviour of both dogs and rhesus monkeys that suggest that an animal deprived entirely of contact with its own species during youth grows up into an asocial neurotic: a sort of behavioural cripple, with its social responses to its fellows distorted or missing altogether.

The various vocal signals used by the different species of *Equidae* have been noted in previous chapters. It seems that the calls are highly individual and mothers and foals in particular can recognize and respond to one another's voice. Some calls have a more general effect, for instance a loud neigh or whinny may alarm the whole herd and set it on the alert or in flight. Others, such as the snort of the fighting stallion or the squeal of the mare in oestrus appear to be either threats or expressions of emotion. In the main however, so far as communications between individuals are concerned, visual signals are more important than sounds.

Horses have a quick eye for slight muscular movements and changes in the posture of their companions and perhaps communicate many of their feelings by signalling in some such subliminal manner. To the human eye horses use five distinctly different facial expressions to suit different circumstances. When threatening to attack, the horse will lay back its ears, perhaps slightly open its mouth and then quickly lunge at its opponent, often missing either by intent or because the warning has been heeded and evasive action taken; stallions use this threat-face when driving their mares and add to its intimidating effect by lowering the head and swinging it menacingly from side to side; in a threat to kick, the laying back of the ears is often accompanied with a swishing of the tail and the raising of a hind

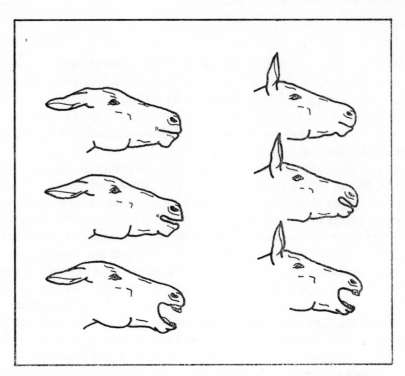

Figure 7. Facial expressions of the horse (threat [left] and greeting [right]).
(After Ewer.)

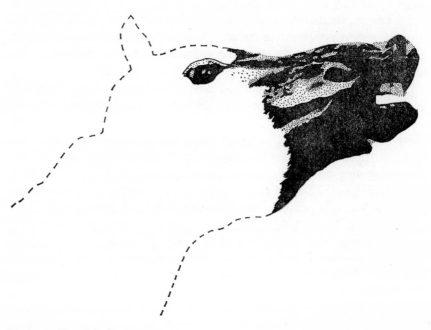

Figure 8. The flehmen posture.

foot. Then there is the greeting-face, with ears cocked forward and the mouth slightly relaxed, which accompanies a friendly encounter that may lead to a touching and sniffing of face and body and perhaps a bout of mutual grooming. Foals when wishing to initiate a grooming session with an older animal will make a sort of champing snapping movement with their jaws; snapping is usually meant to be a submissive expression but it may fail to save a foal from punishment by bad-tempered mares that are unappeased by such a gesture. Yawning is often seen after a rest period or some other pleasurable experience. Finally there is the flehmen posture in which the upper lip is curled back in what has been aptly described as giving the appearance of a careful tasting of smell. The head-raised, lip-curled posture is assumed by the stallion after sniffing at a mare in oestrus and both sexes and foals may behave likewise after smelling at fresh urine or simply in imitation of another animal that is flehming.

Chapter 14

Some Aspects of Horse Breeding

EVEN the greatest biologist Charles Darwin once believed in the theory of telegony, the supposed ability of a female's first mate to influence the progeny of later unions with different sires. At the same period, the first half of the nineteenth century, it was strongly held that during pregnancy various mental impressions received by the dam could affect the developing foetus in her womb: to the extent that a farmer wanting, say black calves would think it sensible to paint his cow byre that colour. And, despite clear evidence to the contrary, such as the fact that after many generations of tail-docking, mares still produced foals with normal tails, it was thought quite likely that acquired characters, such as docked tails, could be transmitted through the germ cells to the offspring.

It is doubtful if such theories and superstitions had much real influence on horse-breeding practices which, in the main, have always been based on some form of selection of the breeding stock. The methods of selection naturally vary according to the circumstances. In the New Forest, where the aim is to produce a useful average type of pony suited to the local environment, the poorer males are weeded out and only selected indigenous stallions are allowed to breed with the Forest mares; in other areas Arab or thoroughbred stallions may be used to upgrade the local stock, or, as in the production of hunters, to produce riding horses of better quality than their dams. On the other hand among the breed societies the dam is regarded as almost as important as the sire, and matings are arranged only after a careful study of the pedigrees of both the male and the female parents. This is particularly the case in the bloodstock industry where the objective is not just to rear numbers of animals of good average ability but rather to produce a few superlative individuals capable of developing outstanding athletic performances under optimal conditions of care and management.

In the non-thoroughbred world, the arrangement of matings is apt to be a casual business, no more than getting a mare in foal to a suitably priced stallion in the vicinity. And these stallions are judged largely on their physical appearance, their conformation and other characteristics that may or may not be heritable. Colour, which is heritable, is of importance in some breeds; Suffolk Punches, Cleveland Bays and Palominos to name but a few; and certain colours may be favoured because they are imagined to go with stamina, courage and other desirable attributes. For many reasons, including the fact that good horses come in all shapes and colours, a breeding programme based on parental physique alone will give disappointing results. And assessment on parental performance may not help over-much either as individual prowess depends so much on factors that are not heritable, among them good management and freedom from disease and injury.

The only valid test that can be applied to breeding stock is to let them prove their ability to get offspring of the required standard of excellence. But this is a time-consuming process: even in the early-maturing thoroughbred it means that a stallion cannot be correctly assessed until he is six or seven years old and his offspring have had the opportunity, as two-year-olds and three-year-olds, of proving their quality on the racecourse. From sheer economic necessity breeders must in the first place select on phenotype, that is on the physical appearance and individual performance of a stud animal, and later check on the genotype, that is the ability to transmit the required qualities, by observing the physique and performance of the young stock. The stud books of the breed societies can help in the selective process and this is particularly true of the thoroughbred, which has behind it two centuries of carefully documented history.

In 1897, Galton, an eminent anthropologist, proposed as a statistical law of heredity that the two parents contributed between them one half of the total heritage of the offspring, the four grandparents one quarter, the eight great-grandparents one eighth and so on. Although faulty in theory, Galton's 'law of ancestral inheritance' provides a rough practical guide for breeders of pedigree stock, both for planning parentage and for assessing the probable capabilities of young stock. Leicester [35] states that it is commonly used by bloodstock breeders to determine the probable staying power of an unraced horse or to estimate the probable distance ability of an unborn foal. Galton's formula definitely does make it possible to separate out potential long-distance and middle-distance horses from the sprinters, which can stay only for distances of under a mile.

89

In 1900 Mendel's laws dealing with the inheritance of contrasted characters were unearthed after forty years of obscurity and brought to the notice of the world. With tremendous optimism, breeders thought that now at last animal matings could be arranged to give mathematically certain results in accordance with the apparently simple ratios of Mendelian expectation. Federico Tesio [59], the successful racehorse breeder, describes his first reading of Mendel's work: 'To me it was a revelation. I had finally understood why two thoroughbred horses, although born of the same sire and dam, in other words full brothers, may turn out to be the one a chestnut and a great runner, the other a bay and a mediocre performer, although both are well built and without apparent faults.'

So far as the inheritance of simple contrasting characters was concerned the Mendelian theory provided satisfactory answers. For instance, in the inheritance of coat colour, chestnut is recessive to all other colours and it can be safely predicted that the mating of chestnut with chestnut will produce chestnut foals; and the inheritance of the other colours can also be forecast with a reasonable degree of accuracy. However it was a different matter when it came to working out the pattern of inheritance of the many factors that go into the make-up of an outstanding racehorse or a good hunter or of any other specialized type of animal. Much of the practical breeder's disillusionment with genetics dates from this period when the first glimmer of understanding of the mechanism of heredity was mistaken for complete comprehension.

Since then, of course, an enormous expansion of knowledge has taken place regarding the structure and chemistry of cells and their chromosomes and genes, as well as in mathematical analysis of genetical processes. The discovery that the basis of hereditary material consists of deoxyribonucleic acid (DNA) is profoundly exciting and altogether so much is now known about inheritance that it comes as something of a shock to realize that the breeder of horses still has to rely on the old traditional practices of selection by phenotype and on progeny testing. This perhaps is inescapable as he is dealing with small numbers of animals of a slow breeding species in which 90 per cent of the genes are probably common to all, perhaps 5 per cent are special to the various breeds and maybe only 5 per cent of the genes remain to account for individual variations from the average standard of performance; and some of those variations will be below rather than above the mean. Nevertheless genetical studies are rewarding if only because they can demonstrate the hazards of breeding that can be avoided.

For example, the potentially lethal disease of haemophilia, which can tragically shorten the life of affected human males, has been found by Archer [5] to occur also among thoroughbred horses. The mode of inheritance is thought to be the same in horse and human, namely through a sex-linked recessive gene carried on the x chromosomes.

The horse has thirty-two pairs of chromosomes of which one pair, xx, is peculiar to the female animal and another pair, xy, to the male. In rare instances, an x chromosome may carry a gene that affects adversely the production of a blood protein essential for the clotting of blood and without which any slight knock or cut may occasion uncontrollable haemorrhage. Because the gene is recessive it can only express its abnormal bleeding effect in the male with his, in this respect, inert y chromosome; in the affected female the one normal x chromosome dominates the recessive gene of the other x chromosome, giving a normal clotting blood. Nevertheless, that affected female is a carrier and can transmit the defect to her offspring.

The affected male is unlikely to survive long enough to reproduce his species and, in the horse, the common chain of transmission of haemophilia is through the carrier mare, which of course appears outwardly quite normal. A carrier mare mated to normal stallions may be expected on average to produce equal numbers of affected and unaffected offspring, that is to say half the fillies will be carriers and half the colts haemophiliacs. It is only by recognition of the defective colts that the carrier mare can be identified and eliminated from the breeding programme, together with her offspring.

Another study of practical importance to the breeder concerns the pattern of inheritance of the many factors to be found in the blood which in some instances can be grouped together as blood types. By the end of the nineteenth century it had been established that either agglutination or lysis of the red cells occurred when human blood was mixed with that of other species and soon afterwards the discovery of the ABO system in human blood showed there were differences between the blood of individuals of the same species that could have the same dangerous effects if unmatched blood was used for transfusion. Naturally the blood types of horse and man differ considerably, but even so there are similarities.

For instance, the discovery that 'yellow baby disease' in humans was caused by the incompatibility of the blood groups of mother and child led a little later to the conclusion that neo-natal jaundice of the foal originated in a similar manner. There are, however, important points of difference between the two diseases. The human disease may occur when a wife possessing a rhesus-negative blood conceives a child with a rhesus-positive blood factor inherited from the father. In such cases the mother may develop antibodies to her baby's red blood cells that can damage them while the baby is still in the womb, causing anaemia and jaundice.

In the equine haemolytic disease, the mare develops antibodies to an incompatible blood group in her foal but these do not pass to the foal *in utero*. Instead they concentrate in the first milk, the colostrum, along with useful antibodies that serve to protect the new-born foal against infection when it leaves the safety of the womb. Thus when blood tests indicate that a mare is likely to produce a haemolytic foal, the disease can be circumvented by discarding the dangerous first milk and for the first thirty-six hours of its life giving the foal an alternative form of nourishment, supported advisedly by colostrum from a safe source, such as a 'colostrum-bank', or perhaps relying on antiserum or antibiotics to protect the foal until it has had time to develop its own defence mechanism against infection. Several different antibodies and antigens have been identified in cases of foal haemolytic disease, which is, however, a relatively rare condition that seems to have a higher incidence among thoroughbreds than among other breeds.

The many genes that determine the various blood factors can combine, in the process of reproduction, in many different permutations, and it is therefore unlikely that any two horses will possess identical blood types. For this reason the character of the blood type provides a useful means of positively identifying an animal and may in future become a standard part of the official description of a thoroughbred, along with its colour, markings and so forth. And, because blood groups are inherited in a Mendelian fashion, they provide a reliable method of resolving cases of doubtful parentage. Scott [51] points out that blood groups fulfil the classic requirements for such investigations, namely, they are developed at birth or soon after; they remain unchanged throughout life; and they are detectable by reliable laboratory tests. Usually a dispute is over paternity. A stallion is excluded as a sire of a foal if both he and the dam lack blood factors present in the foal; or if the heritable blood factors, which he must by the laws of genetics transmit to his offspring, are not present in the foal.

Haemolytic disease appears to be the only equine disease directly associated with specific blood groups. And there is no obvious relationship between blood groups and physical ability, which is not surprising as such attributes as speed and endurance are made up of many different factors, both heritable and otherwise. Resistance to disease is also a quantitative character, influenced both by environment and heredity, and not it would seem related to any particular blood type. However in man some conditions, among them stomach cancer and duodenal ulcer, do have a high correlation with certain blood groups, and an abnormal form of haemoglobin, which is mostly confined to the human races inhabiting the tropical regions, has been shown to give some resistance to malaria. Perhaps in time similar relationships may be found to exist in the horse.

The colour of a horse is one of its most obvious features and it is very understandable that breeders should at times show preference for one hue or another in the belief that it is associated with high performance or a robust constitution. But in fact there is no obvious correlation between the colour of a horse's coat and its working ability. However myths are plentiful, their origins reaching back perhaps into pagan times when horses played an important part both in mundane affairs and in the ceremonies that linked the world of gods and spirits with man on earth. For example, each spring in ancient Rhodes a white horse was harnessed to a burning chariot and cast into the sea in order that it should go to rescue the sun's chariot from its long months of winter weakness. To this day in eastern countries certain colours, markings and hair whorls are thought to bring good fortune, or ill as the case may be, to the rider; and in Britain some people will hesitate to hunt on a black horse, thinking it unlucky, though, in the Middle Ages, black was the preferred colour for a war-horse. Light, washy-coloured horses may be discriminated against because they are supposed to be lacking in stamina; and chestnuts, like red-headed people, are suspected of being rash and over-excitable.

Nothing could be more docile than the Suffolk Punch, which is invariably chestnut – the only colour acceptable in the stud book of the breed. Fortunately chestnut is an easy colour to fix in a breed because it is recessive to all other colours and a chestnut-coloured horse cannot conceal another colour in its genotype; chestnut bred to chestnut will always produce chestnut offspring. On the other hand, there must have been many disappointments before bay could be established as the hallmark of the Cleveland breed because bay is dominant to brown, black and chestnut. Bay horses may therefore conceal the genetic characters for those colours and their progeny may be brown, black, chestnut or bay. Long periods of selective breeding can eliminate the unwanted colours from the genotype. This has been achieved with the Cleveland Bay, which has been developed into a genetically pure bay that will breed true to that colour.

Colour inheritance is not merely a matter of transmission of contrasting dominant and recessive characters to the next generation. There are over

93

a dozen genes affecting the shade of colour and its distribution over the head, neck and body, as well as the appearance of the various white and other markings commonly seen on the legs, face and other parts of the anatomy. The resulting gene interactions can introduce difficulties to some breeding programmes. For instance the palomino pattern, a pale-gold coat with silver mane and tail, is due to dilution of chestnut colour by a gene that functions in such a way that only half the offspring of a Palomino to Palomino mating are likely to show the palomino colour. This colour therefore cannot be fixed in a breed but must be produced either by chance or by mating individuals of suitable genotype that may not themselves be Palominos. Jones and Bogart [31] state that 100 per cent Palominos can be expected from mating a cream-coloured wall-eyed stallion to chestnut mares with silver manes and tails; this mating gives a rather dull yellow colour, which is considered less desirable than the bright gold produced by crossing Palomino to chestnut, though in this case only half the young are Palominos.

The spotted coat of the Appaloosa horse has an even more complicated system of inheritance involving several colour genes and a number of modifying genes. The permutations of all these factors that occur during reproduction result in many different coat patterns, varying from the vividly spotted to the virtually unspotted animal. The latter however will almost certainly display the basic markings that identify the Appaloosa, namely a mottled skin, a marked white of the eye and striped hooves.

Grey is described as a varying mosaic of black and white hairs, with the skin black. As the animal grows older the coat grows lighter in colour. Grey is dominant to all other colours so a grey to grey mating may produce grey, bay, brown, black or chestnut unless, of course, one is dealing with genetically pure greys. A grey horse may become quite white with advancing age but it is still described as grey in accordance with the old adage that there is no such thing as a white horse. This is in fact untrue: a form of albinism does exist giving affected horses a skin and coat almost devoid of pigmentation. The condition is due to a recessive gene acting in conjunction with other genes. It is not possible to fix albinism in the same way as chestnut can be fixed in a breed. The animals are extremely sensitive to sunlight and have other undesirable weaknesses. In its genetically pure form albinism is lethal. When albinos are mated to albinos the foetus that inherits the albino factor in a pure form will die *in utero*: the expected result of such matings is a quarter of the offspring coloured, one half albinos and one quarter never born.

Among mares in general, whatever their colour, about 10 per cent of the foetuses die during the first two months of pregnancy. Probably only a fraction of this loss is due to inherited lethal characters of one sort or another and it would be wrong to exaggerate their economic importance. But inbreeding will certainly concentrate recessive characters in a genotype and an accumulation of lethal factors may well be the reason why fertility is often reduced by inbreeding: the albino provides an extreme example of this potential danger.

Chapter 15

The Horse Crafts

WHEN the horse makes its first appearance as a domesticated animal during the third millennium BC it is as a draught animal, pulling a cart, indicating that already there were men skilled in the quite intricate techniques of the manufacture of wheels and harness. The full exploitation of horse power is largely dependent on these and other artefacts and in view of the supreme importance of horse power in the ancient world it is surprising that during the subsequent two thousand years so little was done either to improve on the primitive method of harnessing a horse to a wheeled vehicle or to devise such comparatively simple but obviously useful articles as saddles, stirrups and horseshoes.

Before the horse was domesticated oxen were employed for haulage, yoked in pairs to a centre pole of a wagon and guided by a rein attached to a copper ring piercing the nose or the upper lip. Then, in Mesopotamia, the onager was tamed for use in the war chariot to which it was harnessed in much the same way as the draught ox was harnessed. But on the onager's narrow shoulders the yoke fitted awkwardly, needing to be held in place by a broad neck-band which in its turn was secured by a strap passing between the forelegs and fixed to a girth. The great disadvantage of the neck-band was the pressure it exerted on the windpipe and the jugular veins when the animal attempted to pull hard. It is estimated that the tractive ability of an animal in this harness is 75 per cent less than the pull that can be exerted when a modern collar or breast-band is worn. A possible advantage of the neck-band was that, with only a nose-ring to steer his notoriously unhandy onagers, the charioteer may well have been thankful at times for its throttling effect to restrain his team and to prevent it from bolting out of his control.

In due course the horse replaced the onager and inherited its harness, except that, instead of the nose-ring, a bit was used; or, in some instances,

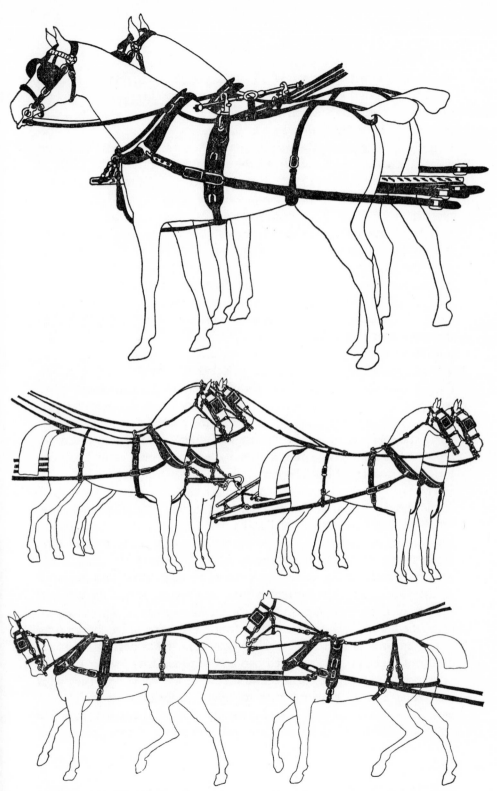

Figure 9. Three types of harness. Top to bottom: curricle harness, four-in-hand coach harness, tandem harness.

a form of dropped nose-band which, when pulled by the reins, pressed on the lower part of the nose and reinforced the stifling effect produced by the pressure of the neck-band on the windpipe and jugular veins. The design of some of the chariots allowed a further measure of control: in the one-man Egyptian chariots the driver would often knot the reins round his waist in order to free his hands for the use of bow or spear; by a shift of his position he could then guide or check his team with the reins, while the alteration of balance in the chariot resulting from his movement would place more or less weight on the yoke and so affect the rate of progress. It is mentioned in chapter 10 that the Chinese had adopted an improved type of chariot harness by the fourth century BC but in Europe it is not until the twelfth century AD that an efficient breast-harness came into general use; also at about this period a draught collar was introduced that took the pull on the shoulders rather than on the neck, and a method of harnessing horses in tandem – all of them simple things but nevertheless they improved enormously the work capacity of horse transport, making it possible to shift far greater loads than ever before and over longer distances. The ancients adhered strictly to the principle of yoking animals together, though with the four-horse *quadriga* often only the two strongest horses were placed under the yoke with the others fastened on each side with ropes, and around half a ton seems to have been the normal maximum load for horse transport. In contrast, Tylden [61] quotes a seventeenth-century report that a cannon weighing four and a half tons could easily be drawn by 'fifteen couples of lusty horses'.

The early horsemen rode to war bareback using the hit-and-run tactics of the thrown javelin or the harassment of arrows shot from a distance, which the mounted archers of Parthia made famous; when man-to-man combat was necessary, they would dismount to fight on foot with spear, axe or sword. About the ninth century BC the Assyrians introduced a cloth or skin-covering for the horse's back which, though viewed with disfavour by the more conservative horsemen, gradually became part of the standard equipment of cavalry in most parts of the known world. This shabrack saved the horse's back to some extent from the friction of bareback riding but it did little to stabilize the rider's seat until it was developed several centuries later into a hair-stuffed pad and provided with leather loops or other primitive forms of stirrups into which the feet could be thrust. This innovation enabled mounted men to fight at close quarters with heavy weapons – thus completely changing cavalry tactics and altering the whole art of war. The metal stirrup took a long time to evolve, coming into general use around the sixth century AD. Perhaps some emotional factor was responsible for the delay: just as the Teutonic tribes of Caesar's time regarded with contempt those who used saddle pads so, one imagines, stirrups must have been considered as a mark of incompetence and degeneracy by men who had been raised from boyhood, almost literally, on the bare back of a horse.

The bit has been used to control the horse from the earliest days of its domestication, at first in the form of a simple bar of horn, bone or wood and then, as copper, bronze and iron became available, in the form of a jointed mouthpiece almost identical with the modern snaffle. The snaffle is a mild bit that permits a horse to extend its neck and gallop on: an excellent thing in open country and where maximum speed is required without too much need to worry about stopping and turning, but its use may be hazardous in other circumstances, especially in the presence of the enemy. At around 300 BC, in response no doubt to the necessity of keeping firm control of the horse in the newly developing technique of close mounted-combat, a more severe bit, the curb, was introduced. The snaffle often was, and still is, used in conjunction with the curb but gradually the single snaffle bridle was relegated to the hunting field and the racecourse. In 1627 Charles I, who was an expert horseman, went so far as to issue an edict that English cavaliers were forbidden the use of the snaffle except 'in times of disport'.

The horseshoe, in the form of a metal rim nailed to the under-surface of the foot to preserve the horn from undue wear, came into use around the beginning of the Christian era; its invention was stimulated perhaps by a number of factors operating at that period. Among them were the increased dependence on the horse for both military and civilian purposes in the Roman dominions in northern Europe where, because of the wet weather and hard going, the hoof is more quickly worn down than in many other areas; the heavier work imposed, including the heavy weight of the iron-clad men, who were replacing the lightly armed skirmishers of former times; and a greater appreciation of the worth of a trained war-horse; a fighting man's competence and safety depended on the battleworthiness of such animals and it was not easy to find satisfactory substitutes for them when they became lame or footsore. As was to be said at a much later period: 'The rider must live only for his horse, which is his legs, his safety, his honour and his reward.'

Shoeing had become fairly widespread by the eighth century and it is uncertain where it originated. Northern Europe is the most probable site of origin for the reasons given above and the most likely originators were the Celtic or Germanic tribes, who were expert iron-workers and also provided a high proportion of the auxiliary cavalry units of the Roman army. They also manned the considerable road-transport system that included a fast messenger service linking the provinces with Rome. The Romans themselves were not a notably inventive people and the idea of the nailed shoe does not seem to have occurred to them, though they did make use of a variety of leather socks and metal plates that were tied or strapped to the feet of horses and mules; these can have had only a very limited practical value on the road. There seems to have been no early interest in the subject in either China or the Middle Eastern countries; in fact in hot dry climates the horn of the foot remains hard enough to withstand moderate work without the protection of metal. For instance, in the sixth century BC the Persians created a regular mounted courier service along the 'Royal Road', reaching from Sardis on the Aegean coast via Nineveh and Babylon to Susa; messengers covered the 1600 miles in a matter of nine days, changing horses every fifteen miles, this distance being about the limit that the unshod equine foot can stand in regular daily work. The steppe nomads are often credited with the invention of any type of horse furniture, but it is doubtful if they would have been much concerned with shoeing: their custom of travelling light and providing several horses for each man, together with the relatively soft going of much of their country will have kept hoof wear to a minimum.

Strangely, the horseshoe still has attached to it some of the magic once attributed to the horse and to the farriers, whose patron saint, St Eloi, possessed the gift of removing a horse's foot from the limb and returning it with a new shoe attached – a great help when shoeing a difficult horse. *The Standard Dictionary of Folklore, Mythology and Legend* [34] states:

> The magic of the horse-shoe may be noted obviously in its manufacture from iron since iron is repellent to witches, evil spirits and other beings which work harm to man. Horse-shoes are placed in chimneys, on the doors of stables, dwellings and churches. Taylor does say of such use in England: half the stable doors do show the horse-shoe. In London many of the west-end houses have one on the doors and there are plenty of churches which use this talisman or have used it. The Devil cannot enter any building that has the horse-shoe over the door. Its use as a good luck charm is common in the United States; luck is enhanced by the chance finding of the horse-shoe. It is efficacious on land and sea: Lord Nelson is said to have had a horse-shoe nailed to the mast of his ship the *Victory*.

The positioning of the horseshoe is important; with the points downwards it acts as a protective device for no malignant spirit can pass under an arch of iron and in heraldry all horseshoes are shown in this fashion. For good luck however the heels should point upwards so that the luck does not run out of the shoe but in this position the anti-demonic effect of the iron arch is lost.

The grouping together of artisans has been a common practice from Neolithic times. For instance in Britain there were a number of stone-axe 'factories' that enjoyed a country-wide trade in their products. Over the ages the crafts grew in number and became organized into separate guilds, many of which were subdivided into brotherhoods, each with a court or governing body that saw to the discipline and well-being of its trade. On the whole this was an advantageous system, leading each trade to feel a strong sense of responsibility for the maintenance of a high standard of skill among its members at a period when society was particularly depen-dent on individual workmanship. Not that mass production was unknown in medieval times: for example, in the twelfth century the Forest of Dean supplied Richard Coeur-de-Lion with fifty thousand horseshoes to equip his knights for the Third Crusade, but each article was handmade and for this to be satisfactory each artisan must have achieved, through a long apprenticeship, a standard level of craftmanship.

Many of the present livery companies of the City of London were founded during the Middle Ages. What surely must be the oldest of the horse crafts, that of the loriners, the makers of bits, spurs and stirrups, established itself as a guild in the forty-fifth year of the reign of Henry III, 1261, for 'the improvement and relief of the Mystery and the honour of the City and the abatement of all frauds and deceits'. It is believed that only a few years later, in 1272, the Worshipful Company of Saddlers received its first charter from Edward I, though the formation of the Company may date back even earlier to an Anglo-Saxon guild of the previous century. The Company once had complete control of all aspects of the saddlery trade throughout England and its court had authority to make search on the premises of all saddlers in the country to see that their wares were well and truly wrought. Later the power of search was restricted to a limit of two miles outside the City of London. This ancient duty is still exercised by the Company four times each year, and the Master may burn any imperfect saddle he finds in Cheapside: and rightly, for there is nothing more harmful to the horse or dangerous to the rider than a badly made saddle. Appropriately the motto of the Company reads, 'Hold Fast Sit Sure'.

The Worshipful Company of Farriers was established as a fellowship by the name of 'Marshalls of the City of London' in 1356; little is known of the fellowship as all its records were lost in the Great Fire of London in 1666 but in 1674 Charles II granted a new charter as a result of a petition from 'the Brotherhood of Farryers within our Citties of London and Westminster that their art and trade is of great antiquity and of great use and benefitt to our subjects for preserving of horses and that diverse and unskilfull persons inhabiting within the liberties of the said Citties have of late taken on them the said Art and Mistery whoe have thereby for want of due knowledge in the right way of preserving horses destroyed many horses'. Among other things, the charter prescribed that no person was to practise the art of farriery until he had served as an apprentice for seven years; and it authorized the court 'to search for, seeke and find out all and every misdemeanour and defective work and medecines'. The farrier of the seventeenth century combined the functions of shoer and horse-doctor and among the Company's Ordinances of 1678 is the following:

... for the better discovery of horses stolne or of horses that have bin hurt or wounded in or aboute any robberies, noe person or person of the said Art or Mistery of Farriers within the said Citties shall dresse or use their means in any cure in the stable of any house or inne but att his publique forge and also no horse shall be shod in any stable but at the Farriers' publique forge (unlesse it be an evill or unruly horse that will not be shod but in a stable).

The Worshipful Company of Wheelwrights was granted its charter by Charles II in 1670, largely in order to sweep away shoddy workmanship 'whereby much mischiefe happnth to people in the Street by falling of Cartes and Coaches and great damage to Merchants and others in theire Goodes as alsoe losse and danger to Gentlemen'. This craft provides a most fascinating study for, as Bennett [7] mentions:

Although the Worshipful Company of Wheelwrights of the City of London has been in existence for only 300 years, yet the 'art and mistery' of the wheel-wright's craft are amongst the oldest known to man. The method of making wheels for horse-drawn vehicles was unchanged in its essentials for 4,000 years, but with the development of first the bicycle and then the motor car, not only did the craft become extinct, but also its very language has been forgotten.

In preserving the ancient lore of its trade the Company performs a service of considerable historical value. Just how valuable can be appreciated by reading Sturt's *Wheelwright's Shop* [56], in which the craftsman describes with exact and loving care every detail of his craft in a way that gives unexpected insight into other matters.

For instance Sturt mentions that the old method of protecting a wheel's rim from undue wear was to nail on strips of iron, and that the intention of thus shoeing a wheel was just the same as that of shoeing a horse; it seems possible that the idea of horse-shoeing derived from this ancient procedure of the wheelwright. And, as a man with a deep understanding of the niceties of his trade, he is astounded at the expertise of the ancient wheelwrights:

Everything about a wooden axle and its wheels seemed to imply a long-settled population. How could nomadic tribes have accumulated, I will not say the experience, but even the material required? It was not any timber that would serve or even any beech; but to get the right stuff involved throwing and 'opening' a tree at the right season, and on the right soil too. Did the wandering barbarians cart a saw-pit along with them, or a stock of seasoning timber, or a stock of it seasoned? Did they take benches, wheel-pits, the requisite axes and chisels and hand-saws? Or, if not, how did the wandering tribes come trailing over Europe? Or how many thousands of years did they spend on the migration, building villages, gathering traditions of handicraft, seeming to settle down, and then off again?

Besides being an integral part of nomadic life on the steppes, horse-drawn vehicles, once an efficient harness had been devised, became as necessary on land as merchant ships are on the seas; in fact, up to the coming of the railways they and the pack animals were the chief carriers of trade and the main means of intercommunication in most parts of the world. In many ways the draught horse was more important than the riding horse, which served man's purpose mostly in war and in sport. But whether in harness or under saddle, horses had to be bitted and shod. It is fair to say that craftsmen have played a major role in shaping the history of the horse and that it is largely through the combined skills of loriners, wheelwrights, saddlers and farriers that the horse has been able to play such an extraordinary part in the history of man.

Bibliography

1 Allen, G. M., *The Mammals of China and Mongolia*, pt 2 (New York 1940), x.
2 Anderson, J. K., *Ancient Greek Horsemanship* (Berkeley 1961).
3 Andrews, R. C., *The New Conquest of Central Asia* (New York 1932).
4 Antonius, O., 'Über Herdenbilding und Paarungseiggentümlichkeiten der Einhufer', *Zeitschrift für Tierpsychologie*, 1 (1937), pp. 259–89.
5 Archer, R. K., 'True Haemophilia in a Thoroughbred foal', *Veterinary Record*, 73 (1961), pp. 338–40.
6 Barmintsev, Y., *The World's finest Horses and Ponies*, ed. R. Glyn (London 1972).
7 Bennett, E., *The Worshipful Company of Wheelwrights of the City of London 1670–1970* (Newton Abbot 1970).
8 Blenkinson, L. J., *History of the Great War – Veterinary Services* (London 1925).
9 Caesar, *The Conquest of Gaul*, tr. Handford, S. A. (London 1951).
10 Camp, C. L. and Smith, N., 'Phylogeny and functions of the digital ligaments of the horse', *Memoirs* (California 1942), XIII.
11 Cole, S., *The Neolithic Revolution*, 5th edn (London 1970).
12 Cole, S., *Animals in Archaeology*, ed. Brodrick, A. H. (London 1972).
13 Cracraft, J., 'Continental drift, paleoclimate, and the evolution and biogeography of birds', *Journal of Zoology*, 169 (1973), p. 455.
14 Crew, F. A. E. and Buchanan Smith, A. D., 'The Genetics of the Horse', *Bibliographical Genetica*, VI (The Hague 1930).
15 Darwin, C., *Variations of Animals and Plants under Domestication* (London 1868).
16 Drower, M. S., 'The Domestication of the Horse', in *The Domestication and Exploitation of Plants and Animals*, ed. Ucko, P. J. and Dimbleby, G. W. (London 1972).

17 Edinger, T., 'Evolution of the horse brain', *Geological Society of America Memoirs*, 25 (1948).

18 Ewart, J. C., *The Penycuik Experiments* (London 1899).

19 Ewer, R. F., *Ethology of Mammals* (London 1968).

20 Fisher, H. A. L., *A History of Europe* (London 1973).

21 Fisher, J., Simon, N. and Vincent J., *The Red Book* (London 1972).

22 Flower, W., *The Horse* (London 1891).

23 Glendinning, S. A., 'A System of rearing Foals on an automatic Calf Feeding Machine', *Equine Veterinary Journal*, 6:1 (1974).

24 Gray, A. P., *Mammalian Hybrids* (London 1971).

25 Hafez, E. S. E., Williams, M. and Wierzbowski, S., 'The Behaviour of Horses', in *The Behaviour of Domestic Animals* (London 1969).

26 Harper, F., *Extinct and Vanishing Mammals of the Old World* (New York 1945).

27 Harrison Mathews, L., *The Life of Mammals* (London 1969), 1.

28 Hayes, M. H., *Points of the Horse* (London 1952).

29 Herodotus, *The Histories*, tr. Aubrey de Selincourt (London 1954).

30 Hopwood, A. T., 'The Former Distribution of Caballine and Zebrine Horses in Europe and Asia', *Proceedings of the Zoological Society of London*, p. 897 (1936).

31 Jones, W. E. and Bogart, R., *Genetics of the Horse* (Michigan 1971).

32 Klingel, H., 'Soziale Organisation und Verhalten freilebender Steppen-zebras', *Zeitschrift für Tierpsychologie*, 24 (1967), English summary.

33 Kurten, B., *Pleistocene Mammals of Europe* (London 1968).

34 Leach, M. and Fried, J., *Standard Dictionary of Folklore, Mythology and Legend* (New York 1949), 1.

35 Leicester, C., *Bloodstock Breeding* (London 1957).

36 Lhote, H., *The Search for the Tassili Frescoes* (London 1958).

37 Lommel, A., *Prehistoric and Primitive Man* (London 1966).

38 Lydekker, R., 'Note on the Skull and Markings of a Quagga', *Proceedings of the Zoological Society of London*, 427:1 (1904).

39 Lydekker, R., *The Horse and its Relatives* (London 1912).

40 Lydekker, R., *The Game Animals of Africa* (London 1926).

41 Mitchell, P. C., *Thomas Henry Huxley* (New York and London 1900).

42 Mohr, E., *The Asiatic Wild Horse*, tr. Goodall, D. M. (London 1970).

43 Neve, C., 'The Chinese Horse', *The British Racehorse*, xxv: 5 (1973).

44 Noble, D., 'The Mesopotamian Onager as a draught animal', in *The Domestication and Exploitation of Plants and Animals*, ed. Ucko, P. J. and Dimbleby, G. W. (London 1969).

45 Oakley, K. P., *Man the Tool-Maker*, 6th edn (London 1972).

46 Pietrément, C. A., *Les Chevaux dans les Temps Préhistoriques et Historiques* (Paris 1883).

47 Phillips, E. D., *The Royal Hordes* (London 1965).

48 Ridgeway, W., *The Origin and Influence of the Thoroughbred Horse* (London 1905).

49 Romer, A. S., *Vertebrate Palaeontology*, 3rd edn (Chicago and London 1966).

50 Salensky, W., *Przewalski's Horse*, tr. Hayes, M. H. and Bradley, O. C. (London 1907).

51 Scott, A. M., 'Red Cell Groups of Horses', *Proceedings of the 3rd International Conferences of Equine Infectious Diseases* (Paris 1972), pp. 384–93.

52 Shortridge, G. C., *The Mammals of South West Africa* (London 1934), I.

53 Simpson, G. C., *Horses* (Oxford 1951).

54 Sisson, S. and Grossman, J. D., *The Anatomy of domestic Animals*, 4th edn (Philadelphia and London 1953).

55 Stirton, R. A., 'Phylogeny of North American Equidae', *Univ. of Calif. Publications of Geology*, 25 (1940), pp. 165–98.

56 Sturt, G., *The Wheelwright's Shop* (Cambridge 1974).

57 Summerhays, R. S., *Horses and Ponies* (London 1971).

58 Tegetmeier, W. B. and Sutherland, C. L., *Horses, Zebras, Mules and Mule Breeding* (London 1895).

59 Tesio, F., *Breeding the Racehorse* (London 1958).

60 Tregear, M., *Animals in Archaeology*, ed. Brodrick, A. H. (London 1972).

61 Tylden, G., *Horses and Saddlery* (London 1965).

62 Tyler, S. J., *The Behaviour and Social Organisation of New Forest Ponies. Animal Behaviour Monographs*, pt 2 (1972).

63 Van Lawick-Goodall, H. and J., *Innocent Killers* (London 1970).

64 Walton, A. and Hammond, J., 'The maternal effects on growth and conformation in Shire horse–Shetland pony crosses', *Proceedings of the Royal Society*, B125: (1938), p. 311.

65 Williams, M., 'The Effects of Artificial Rearing on the Social Behaviour of Foals', *Equine Veterinary Journal*, 6: 1 (1974).

66 Youatt, W., *The Horse* (London 1963).

67 Zeuner, F. E., *A History of Domesticated Animals* (London 1963).

Index

Abyssinia, 41
Achilles, 50
Aden, 58
Africa, 3; colonists introduce horses to, 57;
  desert-bred horses, 55, 64; evolution of
  horse in, 8, 9, 11, 12, 47; introduction of
  horse riding, 51; Islamic conquests, 60;
  wild asses and donkeys in, 26, 32, 36–7,
  38; zebras in, 21, 26, 39–42, 78–80
African horse sickness, 57
African wild ass, 82; *see also* asses
age, gauged from teeth, 18
Akhal-Teke, 74
Alaska, 3
albinism, 94
Alexander the Great, 50
Algeria, 64
Algerian ass, 36
Allan, G. M., 34
Altamira, 23
America, *see* North America; United States
American Saddle Horse, 70–1
American Stud Book, 65
American Trotter, 76
Anatolia, 49
Anchitherium, 6, 9, 12
Andalusian horses, 55, 56, 64
Anderson, J. K., 55, 60
Anglo-Arab, 66
Anglo-Don, 73
antelopes, 20, 65
Antonius, O., 82
Appaloosa, 94
Arab horse, 47; Anglo-Arab bred from, 66;
  as ancestor of English thoroughbred, 62–
  4; development of, 55, 60–2; introduced
  to Australia and South Africa, 57; skulls
  of, 21; Russian horses cross-bred with,
  73, 76; telegony in, 45; used to upgrade
  other breeds, 62, 88

Arabia, 26, 55, 60–2; horses exported from,
  58; wild asses and donkeys in, 32, 34, 37
Archaeohippus, 9, 12
Archer, R. K., 91
Arctic, Russian horses in, 75
Ardennes horses, 76
Armenia, 49
Artiodactyls, 7
Asia, after the Ice Age, 26, 47; evolution of
  horse in, 12; horses used for sport in, 75;
  in Tertiary period, 3; introduction of
  horse riding, 51; native horses, 72, 73–5;
  nomads in, 27, 51; *see also* Eurasia
Asiatic wild ass (*Equus hemionus*), 28, 32–5,
  36, 37, 43, 44; *see also* asses
Asses, 1, 32–5, 36–7; chromosomes, 46;
  colouration and markings, 32, 36, 37, 39;
  distribution after the Ice Age, 26; domestication of, 5; herd behaviour, 82; hybrids,
  43, 44, 45; in Egypt, 60; milk, 38; origins
  of, 21; *see also* African wild ass; Asiatic
  wild ass; donkeys
Assyrians, 49, 50, 98
Astrohippus, 11
Attila the Hun, 55
Australia, 2, 57–8, 62, 80
Aztecs, 56

Babylon, 49, 100
bachelor herds, 79, 80, 81
Badkhyz Reserve, 35
baguales, 56
Baker, Sir Samuel, *The Red Book*, 37
Bakewell, Robert, 68
Barbary horses (Barbs), 62, 63, 64–5
Barmintsev, Y., 74, 75
Bashkir, 74
Basuto pony, 57
battle-axe people, 54

109